How a Little Planning Beats a Lot of Firefighting

Fergus O'Connell

A How To Book

ROBINSON

ROBINSON

First published in Great Britain 2015 by Robinson

A CIP catalogue record for this book
is available from the British Library.

ISBN: 978-1-47211-906-3 (B-format paperback)
ISBN: 978-1-47211-907-0 (ebook)

Typeset in Times New Roman by TW Typesetting, Plymouth, Devon
Printed and bound in Great Britain by Clays Ltd, St Ives plc

Robinson
is an imprint of
Constable & Robinson Ltd
100 Victoria Embankment
London EC4Y 0DY

An Hachette UK Company
www.hachette.co.uk

www.constablerobinson.com

How To Books are published by Constable & Robinson, a part of Little Brown Book Group. We welcome proposals from authors who have first-hand experience of their subjects. Please set out the aims of your book, its target market and its suggested contents in an email to Nikki.Read@howtobooks.co.uk

Fergus O'Connell has a First in Mathematical Physics from University College Cork and is one of the world's leading authorities on project management. His company – ETP (www.etpint.com) – and his project management method – The Ten Steps have influenced a generation of project managers. In 2003 this method was used to plan and execute the Special Olympics World Games, the world's biggest sporting event that year.

Fergus is the author of thirteen business and self-help books. The first of these, *How to Run Successful Projects – the Silver Bullet*, has become both a bestseller and a classic and has been constantly in print for over twenty years. His book on common sense entitled *Simply Brilliant* – also a bestseller and now in its fourth edition – was runner-up in the WH Smith Book Awards 2002. His books have been translated into twenty-two languages.

Fergus has two children and lives in Ireland.

993505403 9

Also available from Constable & Robinson

Top Performance Leadership

Developing Mental Toughness

A Practical Guide To Mentoring

How to Manage Difficult People

How To Make Sales When You Don't Like Selling

Planning and Managing a Corporate Event

For Darin, my indefatigable agent and great friend

'A good plan violently executed now is better than a perfect plan executed next week.' General George S. Patton

Contents

Acknowledgements

A huge thank you, as always, to my redoubtable and tireless agent, Darin Jewell, to whom this book is dedicated.

Nikki Read and Giles Lewis made publishing the book an absolute pleasure.

Jane Donovan was our (yours and mine) copyeditor on this book. This was the first time I had worked with Jane – I hope it won't be the last. Jane did all the heavy lifting so that all I had to do was sprinkle the parsley on top before it went out (if you'll pardon the mixed metaphors).

Finally, a big shout out for the rest of the team at Little, Brown – Clive Hebard, Kate Hibbert, Helena Doree and Andy Hine.

Preface

THE PROMISE OF THE BOOK

As each year goes by, we find ourselves with more and more to do. In work, there seems to be no end of firefighting, constantly changing priorities and always, the threat of downsizing/offshoring/redundancy.

We're told we have to do more with less.

Work smarter, not harder.

But is it possible to do more with less – or is this just an empty phrase passed down from one layer of management to the next?

And what does working smarter, not harder even mean? The first time I heard the phrase used was in 1985 by a boss who, by then, was far out of his depth.

Well, it *is* actually possible to do more with less.

And the key to doing that *is* to work smarter, not harder.

And what that actually means is that we must learn the skill of planning.

Planning is normally thought of as the preserve of large undertakings – great construction projects or huge sporting events or military offensives – and so it is. But planning has a function that is, if anything, at least as valuable.

If we can learn the skill of planning, we can indeed do more with less. We can get much more done in the available time. We will endure a lot less firefighting and unpleasant surprises. In so doing we can have less stress in our lives and be far more productive. We can have much more predictable outcomes to the things we are trying to achieve. And we will indeed be working smarter, not harder.

This is the promise of this book.

DOING WITHOUT DOING

There is a Taoist term called *Wei Wu Wei*. It means 'doing without doing'. While this may sound like a contradiction in terms, doing without doing is exactly what we are going to achieve with this book. We will show that by learning the skill of planning, we can get things done with the least amount of time, effort, resources, money, firefighting, and stress.

And understand too that we're not talking about vast amounts of planning – so-called 'paralysis by analysis'. Rather, a small amount of critical thinking is all it takes to achieve what we're talking about.

You're a busy person. You don't want somebody like me telling you a whole bunch of *extra* stuff you have to do. On the contrary, anything I ask you to do should result in *less* work for you, not more. And – as you'll see – so it will be.

You'll be astonished, I think, at the amount that you can get done in a short space of time. The time you spend planning will be repaid many times over by the time you don't have to spend firefighting.

THE STRUCTURE OF THE BOOK

The book is divided into two parts. Part 1 is for everybody in a job who would like to achieve the promise of doing without doing.

Part 2 will give you the same effect if you run a group/department/ division/organization.

HOW TO USE THE BOOK

It's not going to be enough for you to read the book: you're going to have to *do* things. The book is about trying to change your behaviour – each chapter proposes some new behaviour for you to adopt. Adopt any one of them and you'll see immediate benefit. The more you adopt, the more you'll see benefit. Adopt them all and you will indeed find yourself doing without doing. You will find yourself:

◆ Less stressed

◆ With more time available

◆ Making commitments you know you can deliver on

◆ Getting home on time rather than having to stay late to work

◆ Completing jobs properly rather than in a half-baked or 'fingers crossed, let's hope it will be okay' sort of way

◆ Building a reputation as a person who always gets the job done – calmly and without panic

◆ Having far less firefights and unpleasant surprises happening in your job.

So if I were you, the way I would use the book is like this. Read it a chapter at a time, there's no hurry. Each chapter will suggest some things you should do differently. Start doing these things and witness the benefits. Then go on to the next chapter.

Be sure to hold the gains. After you experience the difference that a particular chapter makes, be sure to continue doing that particular thing until your old way of working is left behind, disappearing in your rear-view mirror.

And finally, it maybe nearly goes without saying – but I'll say it anyway – that while the focus of this book is on work, everything we say here could also be used in your personal life to similar effect.

If all of this sounds attractive, then off we go!

Part 1

Planning for Yourself

1

Why You Wouldn't Cook Dinner Like You Do Your Job

IT'S DINNERTIME

Imagine this. It's about six o'clock in the evening and you suddenly realize you're hungry. You decide to cook dinner. Here's what you do next:

1. You light the gas ring.

2. You look in the fridge to see if there's something to cook.

3. You find there's nothing you like there, so you decide to head down to the supermarket. Hopefully, you turn off the gas ring before you go.

4. You return with some eggs – you're going to make an omelette.

5. You light the gas ring again.

6. Where's the frying pan? Uh oh, it's in the dishwasher and the dishwasher is partway through its cycle. Okay, let's wait until the cycle is over. Turn off the gas again. Go watch TV.

3

7. Finally, the dishwasher cycle is over and you start cooking your omelette. But then you think, 'It'd be really nice to have some fried potatoes with the omelette.' But oh heck, you should have done the potatoes first because they take longer than the omelette.

8. You finish the omelette and put it in the oven to keep warm. Now you start on the potatoes. You're going to have a can of mushy peas with them and happily, you have both enough potatoes *and* the mushy peas.

9. But midway through frying the potatoes, you change your mind. Wouldn't asparagus be really nice instead of mushy peas? Back down to the store again!

10. And so on . . .

Ridiculous, isn't it? It's an episode of *Mr Bean*. You wouldn't do it in a million years. No, of course you wouldn't . . . well, not at home anyway. Not where dinner is concerned.

No, you save that kind of behaviour for work!

HOW MANY TIMES HAVE YOU DONE IT?
The boss calls you in and hands you the project or somebody else gives you something and says, 'This should only take a few minutes . . .' Or you dream up some great idea – wouldn't it be great if we did this? – or some crisis/emergency/firefight breaks out.

What do you do next?

You say 'Sure' or 'Okay' and off you go. Then you start doing stuff . . . Calling meetings, sending out emails, calling people up, contacting recruitment agencies, writing documents and so on, and so on and so on. Before you know it, something unexpected crops up.

And now that's a problem because you've already made a commitment and promised things (when you said 'Sure'/'Okay') and you hadn't expected this thing to happen (because you had thought that nothing unexpected would happen, despite the fact that something unexpected *always* happens) and this firefight that you now find yourself engaged in has a knock-on effect on some other promise or commitment that you made. Which in turn has an effect somewhere else. And so it goes.

Why does this happen? It happens because there's a sequence of events. Everything gets done through a sequence of events; firefights occur when sequences of events collide. Let me explain.

THERE'S ALWAYS A SEQUENCE OF EVENTS

If you were to only take one idea away from this book, take this one. It is that whenever anything gets done – cooking dinner, a small crisis/firefight, a large project, the Olympic Games, the Normandy Landings, anything – it gets done because a sequence of events is identified and carried out.

There is always a sequence of events.

This is how everything gets done.

Knowing the sequence of events after the thing is over is called a post-mortem. Knowing them while you're engaged in figuring them out is called firefighting. Knowing the sequence of events in advance is called a plan.

That's what this book is about – figuring out the sequence of events in advance. Not firefighting, not when the whole thing is all over and lies in a mess at your feet . . .

In advance!

GO DO IT!

There's nothing you need to do in this chapter, just be sure you take away the idea of the sequence of events. It's going to be central to everything we do after this.

PLANNING TIME TAKEN

None so far.

2

Why You Should Only Say 'Sure' When You're Buying Deodorant

As you can see, the book started off gently. In Chapter 1 there was no new behaviour to adopt, just an idea you had to take away. Here, it's a little more demanding because there's something you need to stop doing.

PREDICTING THE FUTURE – IT'S A RISKY BUSINESS

Your boss calls you into his/her office, gathers up the pile of stuff and says, 'Congratulations, you're going to be leading the poison chalice project, and I'm sure it'll be a career-enhancing move for all of us. Oh, and by the way, we don't know much about this project, but it has to be done by this date. You'll have to do it with the team you've got and the budget's already been fixed.'

Or (s)he says, 'Would you mind taking care of this? There's only a couple of hours' work in it and I need it before you go home today.'

Taking on projects – as you do every day in work – is a risky business. It's risky whatever the size of the project – whether some mammoth undertaking all the way down to a seemingly inconsequential request.

It's risky because – if you think about it – you get asked to make a prediction of the future – can you do it by this date/for this budget/ with these people? – and then make that prediction come true. Now, if any of us could actually do that we really wouldn't be doing it at work. Instead, we'd be down at the racetrack or spending our nights in casinos, even buying lottery tickets.

If that wasn't bad enough – and I think you'll agree it is – we often get asked to make these predictions in a very strange way. Imagine your car was acting up and you took it to the garage and what you said to the guy in the garage was, 'I don't know what's wrong with my car, but I'd like you to fix it in the next hour and it'd better only cost fifty euros/pounds/dollars.'

It would be a strange way to ask him to look at your car.

But what would be even stranger would be if he said, 'Sure'.

And when you came back an hour later and drove your car out of the garage, you'd be wondering what he did to your car. Did he do anything? Has he even looked at it? Is the engine going to fall out or catch fire or perhaps explode?

And of course, in the setting of a garage, we couldn't even imagine such a stupid conversation.

But in our kinds of projects, such conversations happen all the time. They're routine. Somebody says, 'Here's the project. I don't know much about it but it has to be done by this date for this budget with these people. Good luck with that.'

And then everyone says, 'Sure'.

MISSILES – BALLISTIC AND CRUISE

The handing over of the project, as we've just described, is a dangerous moment. It's so dangerous that it's like having a missile fired at you.

There are two types of missile – the ballistic missile and the cruise missile. The ballistic missile is launched and we pick it up on our radar screens. It is the explicit handing over of the project as we described in the opening paragraphs.

But there's also the cruise missile – the sneaky one. It gets launched somewhere and suddenly – out of nowhere, it seems – it lands in our lap. Here's an example of a cruise missile. You're at a meeting, say, and somebody asks you, 'How long do you think that would take?' If you're not careful, you'll think up an answer. And if you're not really, *really* careful, you could end up opening your mouth and making a commitment.

Whether the missile is ballistic or cruise, it's dangerous because it carries a warhead. But in our line of business the missile carries a particularly dangerous kind of warhead called the *binary warhead*. A binary warhead contains two things which, once they're kept apart, are harmless but mix them together and they're deadly.

In our case, these two things are:

◆ The request itself – 'Will you do the poison-chalice project?' is an example of a request, and

◆ The 'constraints': these are the idea that even though they've asked you the question, 'How long will that take?' they already know the answer.

  ◆ The project must be finished by a certain date, or

  ◆ It must be done for a certain budget,

  ◆ It must be done with certain resourcing, or

  ◆ The scope of the project has already been fixed, or

  ◆ Some combination of these things.

Now if you try to deal with the request and the constraints at the same time, I hope you can see that potentially, you could end up in a lot of trouble. Because, on the one hand, as you think about the date, you think about all the things you're going to have to do and all the time those things will take. Meanwhile the constraints are telling you that you're not going to get the time.

And you're thinking that you're going to need three highly skilled specialists for a certain part of your project. The constraints are telling you you'll be lucky to get a man and a dog!

In almost every case, the constraints have a tendency to win the argument. And as a result, we can end up committing to doing things that are:

◆ Difficult to do
◆ Impossible to do
◆ Well beyond impossible (if such a place exists).

It has to be said that the number one reason why projects fail is that they were never actually possible in the first place. Somebody said, 'Here's the project. It has to be done by this date or with these resources or for this budget', and everybody just said, 'Sure'.

'SURE' IS A FOUR-LETTER WORD

So if you're going to run your projects successfully, the first thing you have to do is to stop this behaviour. From now on, when a project is handed to you, you're not going to say, 'Sure'. Instead you're going to do what the mechanic or the plumber, or the doctor or the truck driver, or the assistant in the clothes shop or any one of a million other 'normal' trades/industries/professions does, when asked to address a problem. They say, 'We'll take a look at it.' In other words they'll do an examination, come up with a diagnosis and then tell you what's possible and what's not.

This is exactly what you're going to do. Now, in all likelihood, the powers-that-be may be looking for *action* to break out straight away. Once you walk out of your boss's office, (s)he may want to see meetings and brainstorming sessions and teleconferences and documents being written and people developing stuff . . . and all the other paraphernalia of a live project. (S)he may even have uttered the immortal line, 'We don't have time to plan, just go do it.'

It doesn't matter.

All you can say at this stage is, 'We'll take a look at it.' In so doing all you commit to is that you're going to look at the problem and see what's possible and what's not. And with that you walk out, carrying the pile of stuff and turn your attention to Chapter 3.

GO DO IT!

Next time somebody hands you a project, instead of saying, 'Sure', just say 'I'll take a look at it.'

When you do this for the first time, give yourself a reward afterwards – whatever you like, whenever you like, to treat yourself.

After having done it for the first time and treated yourself, keep on doing it. Make it a habit, it's a good one!

PLANNING TIME TAKEN

A few seconds to say, 'I'll take a look at it'. Negligible, to all intents and purposes!

3

What (Exactly) Do They Want?

Having agreed to 'take a look at it' – absolutely the only thing you've committed to doing so far – the next thing you've got to do is to figure out exactly what it is they want. You'll save yourself untold hours of grief if you do this properly. Indeed, it's not an exaggeration to say that if you don't do this right, you could already be well down the road to failure.

There are two things you need to be aware of:
◆ Boxes and clouds, and
◆ Stakeholders and win-conditions.

BOXES AND CLOUDS

The thing you're being asked to do has to be a box; it can't be a cloud. By a box we mean that you put a boundary around the project and say that these things – within the boundary – are part of this project and those things – outside the boundary – are not. Everything within the box is part of the project, everything outside the box isn't.

If you fail to fix this boundary, then you can think of a cloud – a nice big fluffy one. The problem with projects whose goals are cloud-like is that they can't finish (I think you'll agree that this is a pretty serious problem indeed!). They can't finish because we don't know what finish means. With the box, it's almost like we have a checklist. Once we've checked off everything within the box, then we're done. With a cloud we can't do that.

Then, everybody affected by the project will take different views on what the project is delivering. The team will want to deliver as little as possible; everybody else will expect as much as possible. The resulting gulf in expectations will be the cause of great human unhappiness. This is up there with the big project killers and is probably the number two reason why projects fail or get into trouble.

So this is the first thing we must do – we must bound the goal of our project, make it a box. It can't be a cloud.

Perhaps the best way to figure this out is to think about how successful projects end. Think of a dignitary cutting a ribbon to open a new bridge or tunnel or piece of motorway. Or think of a woman breaking a bottle of champagne on the side of ship to launch it. These acts – cutting the ribbon, breaking the bottle of champagne – are symbolic last jobs. They say (to the world) that now that this act has been carried out, now that this job has been done – then this project is over.

So this is what you must also figure out. What is the last job in your project? What is the one thing that, when it is carried out, your project can finally be considered to be over?

STAKEHOLDERS AND WIN-CONDITIONS

If somebody posed you the question, 'What's a successful project?', what would you say? Comes in within the budget? Hits the deadline? Satisfies the customer's requirements?

Sure. These are all facets of a successful project but if you want it in two words, a successful project is 'happy stakeholders'.

Stakeholders are the people who have a stake in the project. More precisely, they're the individuals or groups of people who are affected by the project in some way. We tend to think of the obvious ones – me, my team, my boss, the customer – but generally, if we throw the net a bit wider then we can come up with other stakeholders – people in other departments, groups, organizations.

Every stakeholder has what we can think of as 'win-conditions'. Win-conditions are 'Here's what would make a successful project for me'. In general different stakeholders have different win-conditions. Often win-conditions are diametrically opposed. Also, different stakeholders' win-conditions can have different levels of importance.

In order to get happy stakeholders you have to deliver as many of the win-conditions as possible – ideally all of them – though this may not always be possible.

So the first steps towards happy stakeholders then are:

◆ Figure out who all the stakeholders are

◆ Find out their win-conditions. Do this by asking them. Don't assume you know or that they're the same for every stakeholder. In general they're not.

◆ Get it in writing.

I hope it's clear that if you miss out on certain stakeholders, or you fail to identify particular win-conditions, then the chances of you delivering them by accident are fairly remote. Then you will have stakeholders whose win-conditions haven't been met.

So that instead, you will have met stakeholders' lose-conditions.

Which means you will have unhappy stakeholders.

And this will mean an unsuccessful project.

FIGURE OUT (EXACTLY) WHAT THEY WANT

Here's how to do this. Even on a big project, these two techniques should mean that you should be able to get most of the answers in ten to fifteen minutes. There are two things you need to do:

◆ Figure out the last job in the project

◆ Make a list of its stakeholders and write down their win-conditions.

Then the point in time you chose as the end point of your project should deliver all of the win-conditions. If not, the point in time needs to change or else some of the win-conditions must change.

Here are a couple of examples to show you what this would look like.

Example 1

Suppose your project is to run a job advertisement. What event marks the end of that project?

Thank you for using Gloucestershire Libraries

Card number: 6726

Items that you have borrowed

Title:
How a little planning beats a lot of firefighting
ID: 9935054039
Due: 08/01/2019

Total items: 1
Account balance: £0.00
18/12/2018
Borrowed: 1
Overdue: 0
Reservations: 1
Ready for collection: 0

Gloucester Library - 01452 426973
Have you tried our Library App

Well, maybe it's when the advertisement runs in the paper, but perhaps we wouldn't really regard that as a successful ending to this project. Maybe it's more about whether we get fifty résumés or application forms in, in response to the advertisement? Or maybe it's not about the number of résumés but the quality of them. Do we get five good ones? Or maybe it's about whether the advertisement gets us somebody we can hire? Or is it about whether that person turns out to be any good, so that the event that marks the end of the project is actually the successful completion of the six-month probationary assessment of Charlie, the guy we hired in response to the advertisement?

I hope it's clear that I'm not saying one of these endings is right and all the others are wrong. All of them are possible valid endings. What's important, though, is that all the stakeholders are agreed on the ending that has been chosen.

Make a list of all of the stakeholders and their win-conditions. Here it is.

Stakeholder	Win-conditions
Us	◆ Run ad that reflects well on the company and doesn't upset anybody. It also should communicate why the job on offer is so attractive that you'd have to be mad not to apply.
Our boss	◆ The ad sends out a positive message about the company.
Existing employees	◆ Doesn't upset anybody – uses only material in the public domain. ◆ Sends out a message that the company is one that people want to work for.

Stakeholder	Win-conditions
Potential employees	◆ Sends out a message that the company is one that people want to work for.
Our customers	◆ Sends out a message that the company is expanding, and is a good organization to do business with.

Now we can pick any point in time that will deliver these win-conditions.

Example 2

Suppose our project is to develop some kind of product (it doesn't particularly matter what kind).

To apply our method to this project, we begin by asking, 'What event marks the end of this project?'

Doing this for real, we might do it in conjunction with the stakeholders or we could do it on our own and get agreement from the stakeholders afterwards. Either way works.

Just as with the 'run-a-job-advertisement' project earlier, there are several possible endings to this particular project. The project could be over:

◆ When the product leaves the Product Development department, or

◆ When it has sold in small quantities – some kind of limited customer release, or

◆ When the first year's worth of revenues are in, or

◆ Several other points.

Let's assume that here, the stakeholders agree that the plan we are developing is for the development of the product only, that anything related to sales is the subject of a separate plan. Thus, we are saying that the project is over when the product leaves the Product Development department.

In terms of who the stakeholders and what their win-conditions are, here's a possible list (in no particular order):

Stakeholder	Win-conditions
Project Manager	◆ Project completes on time, within budget and makes the other stakeholders happy ◆ Team enjoy the project ◆ Interesting piece of work ◆ Makes you look good
Head of Product Development	◆ Project completes on time, within budget and makes the other stakeholders happy ◆ Makes him look good
Team	◆ Same as Project Manager, plus ◆ No insane working hours to get the project done ◆ Interesting work ◆ Makes them look good
CEO	◆ Product makes the company lots of money ◆ Gain market share ◆ A product to be proud of – good reviews by those who matter ◆ Make him look good to the Board
Finance department	◆ The product stays within budget and adds so much profit to the company

Stakeholder	Win-conditions
Marketing department	◆ A product to be proud of – good reviews by those who matter ◆ Gain market share ◆ Make them look good
Sales department	◆ Project meets the release date that sales have already announced! ◆ Product sells in shedloads ◆ Big commission for sales people
Rest of the company	◆ Makes the company more secure by increasing its profitability ◆ A product to be proud of
Our customers	◆ A product that meets a real need that they have and they will want to buy
Company shareholders	◆ Grow market share ◆ Meet profit targets

And finally, will the point in time we have chosen deliver all of the win-conditions? Well, provided we:

◆ Deliver a good product
◆ Bring the project in on time and within budget
◆ Don't have the team working insane hours,

then we will meet the win-conditions of

◆ The Project Manager
◆ The Head of Product Development
◆ The team
◆ The customers.

Note that we will not meet all of the financial/sales/marketing win-conditions. *This is a really important point.* The plan that we are going to build is not intended to meet those win-conditions. These win-conditions will require some separate financial/sales/marketing plan. These points, i.e.:

◆ Here's what we're doing on our project

◆ Here's what we're not doing

◆ Here's what would need to be done to meet these other win-conditions

are really important.

They need to be made clear to all of the stakeholders at the outset otherwise we will have a situation where some stakeholders will start out the project with unreasonable expectations. Then, in our example, we could have the most successful product development project in the history of the world and we would still end up with unhappy stakeholders. And remember, unhappy stakeholders equals unsuccessful project.

By making clear to our stakeholders – at the outset – what the project will do and what it *won't* do, we avoid this trap. We document all of this in some document or other and then we're ready to proceed to the next step. The stakeholders may be jumping up and down at this stage looking for action. It doesn't matter – we're still carrying out our examination. We've still got our head under the bonnet of the car!

GO DO IT!

Do what we've described before on a project of your own, i.e.

◆ Figure out the last job in your project

◆ Make a list of its stakeholders and write down their win-conditions.

Then the point in time you chose as the end point of your project should deliver all of the win-conditions. If not, the point in time needs to change or else some of the win-conditions must change.

Give yourself no more than fifteen minutes initially and see how much you get done. Then, if you need a bit more time to finish it off, do that.

PLANNING TIME TAKEN

You could get a lot done in fifteen minutes. I'm not saying that you could always get this done for every huge project that came your way in fifteen minutes – though you could. Rather, it's that for an investment of fifteen minutes so far, you get – I hope you'll agree – a huge payback.

When I do this on courses with people, they almost always find more stakeholders than they originally thought. Good to find that out early in the project. What you don't want is that late in the project somebody steps out from behind a curtain and says, 'I'm a stakeholder' – and you then have to say, 'Who are you and what do you want?'

People also often find that the point in time that they thought was the end of their project isn't necessarily the end; it may be something else. Good to find that out too.

Finally, what about for very small projects or seemingly innocent requests – 'Can you take a quick look at this' kind of thing?

Well, even if all you did was make a list of the stakeholders, if you suddenly find you're into twelve of fifteen stakeholders, this is nature's way of telling you that this may well not be as simple as everybody thought.

Good to find that out too before you go and make some commitment that turns out to be impossible to deliver on.

Notice too that after you've made a list of stakeholders once, this can become your standard checklist of stakeholders each time you start a new project.

So – fifteen minutes so far . . . Let's press on and see what we have to do next.

4

What Do You Have To Do?

Now that you've understood what you're being asked for – the goal – the next thing to do is to figure out what jobs must be done to achieve this. This means that you're going to build the sequence of events or – more simply – a list of jobs. If the goal is your destination, the sequence of events is your journey.

To do that, there are some basics you need to know. The first of these is to understand about two quantities – duration and work.

DURATION AND WORK

◆ **Duration**, sometimes also called **Elapsed time**, is *how long* a particular job is going to take. It is measured in the normal units of time – hours, days, months, and so on. The normal duration of a football match, for example, is ninety minutes.

◆ **Work**, sometimes called **Effort**, is how much work is in a particular job. It is measured in units like man-days, person-hours, person-years and so on. The work in a football match, if we count 2 teams of 11, a referee, two linesmen and a fourth official is 26 times 90 minutes, i.e. 26 times 1.5 hours=39 person-hours.

Durations are important because they enable you to figure out *how long* all or part of a project will take. If you figure out all of the individual task durations, string all of the tasks together, showing what can overlap and what can't, then you end up with the total duration of the project.

But if we want to know what size a project is or what a project will cost or how many people are needed, then duration won't tell you any of that. For this you need to know how much work is going to go into each task. Then, for example, if you did want to know the budget, all you would need are daily rates and then you could figure out what the project is going to cost, i.e. its budget. But we'll get to that. First, let's talk about how to do this estimation properly.

ESTIMATING PROPERLY

The difficulty with estimating is that you have to predict the future, something that nobody can do with 100 per cent certainty. The best you can hope for here is that the error in your prediction will be as small as possible.

There are two things you can do to help you. One is that you can record what happened on previous projects – how long particular tasks took, how much work was involved in them, what they cost and so on – and use this information when you come to plan your next project. (We'll talk about how to do this painlessly in Chapter 8, page 75.)

However, whether you have comparable information from previous projects or not, the key to getting the prediction as right as possible is *detail*. By breaking down the work to be done into small elements of detail, you are less likely to miss vital elements of the project.

Here's our method:

1. Involve the people who are going to do the project, i.e. the team, in the estimating. If they're not all available or haven't yet been assigned or hired, maybe a subset of them is available. If not, get somebody to help you – the worst thing you can do is to do this by yourself.

2. Identify the big pieces of work to be done in the project, the bits that get you from the start to the end (there's no need to be too accurate at this point, broad brushstrokes are fine). It may be that your organization has a standard lifecycle that it follows for projects and if that's the case, follow that. If not, just ask yourself what are the big lumps of work that must be done to get you from the start to the end.

3. Now, within each of these big pieces of work, identify the detailed jobs that have to be done. Break everything down such that each job you identify is between one to five days' duration or one to five person-days of work.

4. Be as specific and concrete as possible, i.e. rather than saying 'requirements gathering' say 'Charley meets with the IT people for two days to explain his requirements'. Write up the plan as if you were writing it for a ten-year-old. In other words, if your ten-year-old son/daughter/nephew/niece couldn't understand it, you haven't done it right and so you need to be more specific.

5. Where you don't know something, make an assumption. The big problem in estimating a project is that you don't have all the facts, all the knowledge. Assumptions are powerful because you

make up facts. If you come to a piece of the project and say, 'I haven't a clue about this', then just make up something. Perhaps you don't know how much testing there will be in your project because you don't know how many errors you're going to find when you come to test it? No problem, just make an assumption – assume three rounds of testing or thirty-three (or whatever). If you have some information from previous projects to guide you then that's great but otherwise just make up something that seems reasonable. You will see examples of assumptions later in this chapter (pages 31–33).

6. Use cause and effect: this means that jobs don't exist in isolation. Once you write down one job, it triggers other jobs. So keep asking the question, 'What happens next?'

7. List all the jobs in a structure that shows the project as being made up of the big pieces of work, which in turn are made up of the smaller pieces. You'll see one of these structures in the example below.

8. Finally, notice what you're doing when you estimate is that you're trying to come up with all of what you might call the parameters of a job. These are:

◆ The job itself
◆ What other jobs it depends on
◆ How much work is involved in that job
◆ How long that job will take (its duration)
◆ How much the job will cost (its budget)
◆ Who's going to do it?
◆ What is their availability?

It's a lot of stuff to try to estimate all at once. For this reason, I find it better at this stage just to focus on *some* of those things. I would suggest that at this stage, you focus on the first four, i.e.:

◆ The job itself
◆ What other jobs it depends on
◆ How much work is involved in that job
◆ How long that job will take (its duration).

Leave the others for a later chapter.

A bad example
Opposite is a piece of a plan with estimates.

On the face of it, maybe it looks okay – looks like a plan, smells like a plan, must *be* a plan.

But it isn't. This plan is a crock in that it breaches almost all the rules we outlined in our method. One problem is that the level of detail is, in general, not detailed enough. But the single biggest problem here is that the tasks aren't clear – they're not concrete. What does 'Module F' mean, for example?

A good example
I'm assuming that very few of the people reading this were around at the time of the Normandy Landings on D-Day, 6 June 1944. And I'm also assuming very few readers have a military background qualifying them to plan this project. However, let's see how we would have done if we had been handed this project. Let's plan a little piece of it.

ID	❶	Task Name	Duration	Start	Finish	Predecessors	Resource Names
1		SDK Development	55 days	Tue 01/05/01	Mon 16/07/01		
2		Core–PC Build	39 days	Tue 01/05/01	Fri 22/06/01		
3		clean up core	10 days	Tue 01/05/01	Mon 14/05/01		DevLead,Dev1,Dev2
4		Module A	5 days	Tue 15/05/01	Mon 21/05/01	3	Dev1
5		Module B	15 days	Tue 15/05/01	Mon 04/06/01	3	Dev2
6		Module C	10 days	Tue 15/05/01	Mon 28/05/01	3	Dev3
7		Module D	10 days	Tue 01/05/01	Mon 14/05/01		Dev4[50%]
8		Module E	5 days	Tue 01/05/01	Mon 07/05/01		Dev5
9		Module F	2 days	Tue 05/06/01	Wed 06/06/01	5	Dev2
10		Module G	10 days	Thu 07/06/01	Wed 20/06/01	9	Dev2
11		Module H	15 days	Tue 29/05/01	Mon 18/06/01	6	Dev3
12		User Manual	30 days	Tue 01/05/01	Mon 11/06/01		Dev4[50%]
13		Release Notes	2 days	Thu 21/06/01	Fri 22/06/01	4,5,6,7,8,9,10,11	Dev1,DevLead,Dev2
14		PS2 Stream	49 days	Wed 09/05/01	Mon 16/07/01		
15		Optimize Module C	15 days	Wed 23/05/01	Tue 12/06/01	8FS-4 days,6FS	Dev5[90%]
16		Optimize Module D	25 days	Wed 09/05/01	Tue 12/06/01	7FS-4 days	Dev6
17		PS2 release notes	1 day	Mon 25/06/01	Mon 25/06/01	15,16,2	Dev5
18		Build Demostream	8 days	Thu 05/07/01	Mon 16/07/01	55	Dev5

Figure 4.1: Plan with extimates

Using step (2) of our method – Identify the big pieces of work – here's a possible breakdown:

1. Start

2. Get soldiers

3. Ship them to just off the Normandy coast

4. Have them get ashore

5. Get past defences to objectives for first day

6. The end.

Now let's (arbitrarily) take item 4 and break it down further:

4.1. Put soldiers in landing craft

4.2. Run landing craft in to shore

4.3. Open bow door

4.4. Soldiers wade through surf and reach dry land.

And then here's our sequence of events:

Task	Dependency	How much work?	How long?
4.1 Put soldiers in landing craft	Item 3	Assuming 30 soldiers in a landing craft and each one takes 2 minutes to board, then 1 person-hour	Assume 3 board simultaneously – note that will need 3 rope ladders per landing craft to do this, then 20 minutes
4.2 Run landing craft in to shore	4.2	Assume the distance is 2 miles and knowing the speed of the landing craft is 5 miles per hour, then 24 minutes for 30 people=12 man-hours	24 minutes
4.3 Open bow door	4.3	30 people for 1 minute=½ man-hour	1 minute
4.4 Soldiers wade through surf and reach dry land	4.4	Assuming this is being done under heavy enemy fire, that the distance is 200 yards and people do it as quickly as possible. How long to wade through 200 yards of shallow surf – do experiment to find out. In the meantime, assume 6 minutes. Six minutes for 30 people=3 man-hours.	6 minutes
TOTALS		16½ man-hours	51 minutes

Now, some day I hope a military person will read this and maybe correct all the flaws in it. In the meantime I think we haven't done badly at all. The 'How much work?' column is probably not particularly relevant in a project like this – I presume people weren't too concerned with the *financial* cost – but notice the things we found out.

The issue of how many ladders there are per landing craft is very important. This will determine how quickly we can fill the landing craft. So too is the speed at which heavily laden men can wade through surf. An experiment on this will provide vital information, i.e. there's something we should/can do early in our project to provide us with valuable information. (Many projects have similar issues where, if we schedule the project such that we do some work early, we can find out valuable knowledge that can then be used to replace our assumptions.) Finally, knowing whether the duration of this piece of the project is 51 minutes or not is crucial in terms of determining when to launch the landing craft. This will be tied to sunrise time, daylight calculations and tides.

You may argue that I picked an easy one – that I should have chosen 5 'Get past defences to objectives for that day'. So, okay, let's pick that one:

5. Get past defences to objectives for that day

   5.1 Get past defences on the shoreline and the beach

   5.2 Get past defences at the back of the beach

   5.3 Get off the beach to that day's objectives.

Now, let's take one of these – arbitrarily the first one – and come up with the sequence of events. (This time we'll omit the calculations of man-hours.)

Task	Dependency	How long?
5.1	4.4	Assume that the only defences on the shoreline and beach are 'hedgehogs' – cross pieces of girders welded together. These, plus machine gun shooting from the back of the beach. Will have to do aerial reconnaissance to confirm what obstacles are there. Should the obstacles be mined, will have to get the mines cleared before the soldiers go ashore. If impossible to ascertain, should assume they are mined. And if the concrete machine gun emplacements haven't been destroyed by the earlier bombardment, won't be able to do anything about them. Beach is, say, 200 yards wide at this point. Do experiments to see how long for a heavily laden soldier to cross 200 yards of sandy beach. In the absence of this, say 5 minutes. Plus allow several blocks of time for being pinned down – say, 3 blocks of 5 minutes each. Total=20 minutes to get to the back of the beach.

Presumably somebody also did calculations about how many soldiers might be needed to cross the beach given a proportion of them would be killed or wounded in trying to do so. Maybe military people have rules of thumb for things like this. In their absence we could do these calculations by making assumptions.

There you go – that's how we estimate properly. If we can do it for this particular project, wouldn't you agree that the same method could be applied to any project?

WHAT ABOUT PROJECT MANAGEMENT SOFTWARE TOOLS?

If you're involved in this business of planning projects then, sooner or later, the subject of a project management tool will come up. Which one to choose, which is the best, should we pick Microsoft Project, or a free one off the Internet, or do we need an enterprise-wide project management tool?

Relax! People built the Pyramids without paper . . . D-Day was planned without a computer . . .

To do anything you need two things – a recipe and a set of tools. This book is about a recipe. Once you know the recipe, you know how to cook the dish. Then you can find a tool or set of tools that will help to make your life easier when you're cooking.

In terms of choosing a tool then my advice would be to use the simplest tool that gets the job done. So, if you can put the plan on a piece of flipchart paper or a whiteboard, do it. Moving up from that, you write the plan in a document on a computer. And moving up from that again you could put the plan into a spreadsheet. Or you can get yourself Microsoft Project or a Microsoft Project type tool, if you feel that will help.

All of these tools, whether you pay for them or not, have strengths and weaknesses. This is true of even the big, expensive, enterprise-wide tools. For example, MS Project does some things wonderfully well (e.g. enabling the building of the list of jobs) and is woeful at other things (e.g. I'm not convinced it calculates the Critical Path correctly – which is why we're not going to worry about that here!).

I believe the only way you can choose a tool is to try it out. Find out where it's strong and whether you can live with its weaknesses. If you feel that you can live with the weaknesses, then use the tool. Otherwise try another one.

In general, I would say only move to a more complex tool if you find that the limitations of the simpler one are causing you a problem. You could also use a combination of tools.

CALCULATING THE BUDGET

We should also talk very briefly about calculating the budget, just in case you're ever asked to do that. Here's how to do it and all you need to know:

Each job in your plan will have an associated cost. This cost can come about in one of three ways:

◆ Labour only – The cost of this job is the work (in, say, man-hours or man-days) multiplied by the hourly or daily rate, as appropriate. Where do you get this hourly or daily rate? Go ask the Finance people. If they can't give it to you, make some kind of assumption. A common assumption would be to say that the daily rate should be two to three times the daily salary.

◆ Labour plus other costs – The cost of this job is the labour cost (as described above) plus other costs – things like travel, hotels, equipment, software, consumables, raw materials and so on. How can you estimate these? Three possibilities – ask a supplier, go look on the Internet or make an assumption.

◆ Subcontract – You are going to pay some supplier a fee to get this job done. In general, in this situation, you don't care how much work the supplier puts into it since they are getting their fee. What you *do* care about, though is *how long* the job is going to take, i.e. its duration and when it will actually be done.

◆ In addition, it is very likely that you will have to devote some time to managing the subcontract – meetings with the supplier, answering questions and emails, perhaps having to push them if they are not performing and so on. Estimate this in person-days, cost it as described above and add this amount to the supplier's fee to give you the final cost of the subcontract.

Adding up the budgets for all the individual jobs gives you the budget for the entire project. It's as easy as that.

GO DO IT!

Now do what we've described above on a project of your own, i.e. apply the method and build the sequence of events. Figure out:

Big chunks

◆ For each chunk, little jobs
◆ For each job, figure out work in person-days
◆ For each job, figure out duration and show this on a chart.

Just to help you, here's another example of what that would look like. This is a possible piece of a plan related to the user testing of an IT system.

Take no more than forty-five minutes initially and see how much you get done. Then, if you need a bit more time to finish it off, do that.

	Depends on	Work (in person-days)	Duration	Who	Availability	Days 1 2 3 4 5 6 7 8 9 10 11 12 13 14 15
Project X						
1 Requirements						
...						
2 Design						
...						
3 Build the system						
...						
4 IT test the system						
...						
5 Users test the system		12				
5.1 First test run		3	3	Users	Full-time	
5.2 IT fix the errors	5.1	2	4	Charlie	Half-time	
5.3 Second test run	5.2	3	3	Users	Full-time	
5.4 IT fix the errors	5.3	1	2	Charlie	Half-time	
5.4 Final test run	5.4	3	3	Users	Full-time	

Figure 4.2: Another piece of a plan with estimates

PLANNING TIME TAKEN

I hope you can see that you could get a lot done in forty-five minutes.

◆ You'd plan a small project completely in that time.

◆ For a big project you obviously wouldn't do that, but you would find out so much. You would uncover so many potential firefights and you would defuse them so that they would never trouble you. The time invested in planning would be repaid many times over by the time you *wouldn't* spend firefighting.

◆ And out in the real world of your job, you may not get all the time you need to fully plan a project. Maybe somebody *does* need an answer by four o'clock today or there's some other deadline or important person shouting for something. But even in fifteen minutes . . . half an hour . . . forty-five minutes, you could find out enough about a project to prevent yourself from committing to something daft. And wouldn't that be a fine thing indeed?

◆ So whatever happens, ignore the idiots who say, 'We don't have time to plan it, just go do it'. They are just that – idiots! Grab yourself whatever little bit of planning time you can and then reap the rewards.

5

Who's Gonna Do It?

SUPPLY AND DEMAND

Like many things in life, getting your project done can be thought of as a problem in supply and demand. The demand comes from the work to be done – the person-days – the stuff you did in the last chapter. Supply comes from the people to do the work – that's what you're going to learn here.

In theory your job is really, really simple. If there are 100 person-days of work to be done, there had better be 100 person-days of people to do the work. This clean and simple view of the world tends to get messed up by two factors. First that the demand has a tendency to go up as stakeholders ask for more things, extra things: 'Can it do this?', 'I thought I was going to get that'.

Then, if that wasn't bad enough, the supply has a tendency to go down as we never seem to have enough people to do all the work. Most of your project will be about the struggle to keep these two quantities in balance. If they go out of balance, and they stay out of balance, then the whole project will crash and burn.

To be completely precise, we should really say 'resources' here, rather than just people. Sometimes your project may require other resources, such as equipment, materials, use of a production line, travel and so on. However, since in most projects it's the people resources that are the problem, this is what we focus on.

By factoring in these things, you add the other 'parameters' to your plan:

◆ Who's going to do it?
◆ What's their availability?

WHO'S GOING TO DO IT?

Add two more columns to your plan. In the first one write down who's going to do the work, i.e. write down the people's names. If you don't know who these people are yet because they haven't been identified or hired or assigned, then write down a description of the kind of skill or person you need – for example, 'Web designer', 'Electrician' and so on.

Remember too that you may need extra jobs in the plan to do with finding these people and bringing them on board. These might be tasks such as running job advertisements, talking to recruitment consultants, doing interviews, making job offers, negotiating with people from other parts of your organization and so on. They could be substantial pieces of work on their own right, so don't forget about them.

WHAT'S THEIR AVAILABILITY?

Availability (or the lack of it) can have a profound and catastrophic effect on your project. To give you a sense of just how catastrophic, look at this simple example.

Say there's one job in your project that you've estimated to be ten person-days; Charlie's going to do it and he's available full-time, i.e. five days per week. Thus the job will take two weeks.

Now suppose Charlie was only available one day per week. Then the job is going to take ten weeks. And that's *at least* ten weeks because you've also got to allow for the fact that Charlie has to put down the job and then come back to it a week later, getting his head around it again.

The drop from five days per week to one day per week may not seem all that significant, but that one small thing can potentially delay the project by two months (eight weeks – the difference between ten weeks and two weeks).

And that's one of Charlie's jobs. So, is this happening on all of Charlie's jobs? Yep, there's a good chance it is. And is this a very unusual phenomenon I'm describing? Absolutely not! The problem of lack of availability, of too much to do and not enough time to do it, of too much so-called 'multitasking', is one of the huge problems in work today.

So, in short, you need to know people's real availability. If you're in any doubt about that, you need to do a Dance Card for them.

A *what*?

DOING A DANCE CARD

The term 'Dance Card' is a reference to those more genteel times in the eighteenth and nineteenth centuries where, when a woman attended a dance or a ball, she was given a little card. On it was a list of the tunes that the band or the orchestra was going to play. To dance with a particular woman, you wrote your name against a particular dance on her Dance Card. Thus the Dance Card was a booking system.

One way to think about the problem of overload is that you've gone and overbooked yourself. Here's an example of a Dance Card.

It shows that over the next six weeks, in a period of thirty working days, somebody has forty-two days' work to do. If you'd like a fill-in-the-blanks spreadsheet for doing Dance Cards, email me at fergus.oconnell@etpint.com and I'll send you one.

So, figure out the real availability of the people on your project and put that in the last column on your plan. Notice too that these availability figures could affect – as in, lengthen – the durations you've identified in Chapter 4. But that's okay: it simply means your plan is becoming more realistic, which is exactly what you want.

(Just as an aside, if you find on one of your projects any of the following symptoms:

◆ Jobs are not getting done
◆ People are working longer and longer hours
◆ Projects are falling further and further behind

then there's a good chance that the reason for this is lack of availability. A Dance Card will check this for you – it could also possibly ruin your whole day!)

#	Project	Basis	01/11	08/11	15/11	22/11	29/11	06/12	Total
1	Project Y wind-down	2 dpw	2	2	2	2			8
2	Meeting with customer	1 day	1						1
3	PLC conference	3 days			3				3
4	Support of project X	0.5 dpw	0.5	0.5	0.5	0.5	0.5	0.5	3
5	Reviews of other designs	4 days	1	1	0.5	0.5	0.5	0.5	4
6	Admin/Inbox/Interruptions	1.5 hpd	1	1	1	1	1	1	6
7	Training others	1.5 hpd	1	1	1	1	1	1	6
8	Support of Project Z	1 dpw	1	1	1	1	1	1	6
9	Holidays	5 days				5			5
	Available	30 days							
			7.5	6.5	9	11	4	4	42
	Notes:								
	(1) 'dpw' = days per week								
	(2) 'hpd' = hours per day								
	(3) All figures in person-days								

Figure 5.1: Dance Card

EXAMPLE

Here's the example from the previous chapter with the 'Who' and the 'Availability' added.

HERDING CATS

Just one final point: if the project involves more than just yourself, i.e. other people also have to do work on it, then you need to add in some extra time to allow for this.

Just because you identify all the jobs and find people to do them doesn't mean they're going to get done. Somebody needs to act as the ringmaster, the conductor of the orchestra; somebody needs to 'Herd the Cats'.

To allow for this, put one extra job into your plan. Call it 'Project Management' (which is what it is) or 'Herding Cats' (or whatever you like). Calculate its effort as being 10 per cent of the total effort of the rest of the project. Show its duration lasting for the duration of the project. Make sure you have enough availability to provide this extra 10 per cent.

GO DO IT!

Now do what we've described above on a project of your own, i.e. add the two extra columns – 'Who' and 'Availability'. If you're in any doubt about anyone's availability, make a Dance Card for them.

It shouldn't take you more than twenty minutes to do this, unless it's a very hefty project indeed, in which case give it the time it needs.

	Depends on	Work (in person-days)	Duration	Who	Availability		Days 1 2 3 4 5 6 7 8 9 10 11 12 13 14 15
Project X							
1 Requirements							
...							
2 Design							
...							
3 Build the system							
...							
4 IT test the system							
...							
5 Users test the system		12					
5.1 First test run		3	3	Users	Full-time		
5.2 IT fix the errors	5.1	2	4	Charlie	Half-time		
5.3 Second test run	5.2	3	3	Users	Full-time		
5.4 IT fix the errors	5.3	1	2	Charlie	Half-time		
5.4 Final test run	5.4	3	3	Users	Full-time		

Figure 5.2: Plan with 'Who' and 'Availability' added

PLANNING TIME TAKEN

So far you've spent less than an hour and a half on your project. I mean, really, when was the last time a firefight took you just ninety minutes to sort out?

And at the risk of sounding like a broken record, those ninety minutes will be repaid many times over by time you don't have to spend firefighting.

◆ You might have saved yourself a day's firefighting (eight hours) by investing this ninety minutes. That's a payback of more than 500 per cent.

◆ You might have saved yourself a week's firefighting (forty hours). That's a factor of twenty-six payback.

◆ You could have saved yourself a month's firefighting. That's about 160 hours (if we only count working ones – it's much more if you include your home life) saved. In other words, a factor of more than 100 – 10,000 per cent!

◆ You might have saved yourself *more* than a month's firefighting by the simple fact of not committing to something that was impossible in the first place.

So, does planning pay back?

Does planning pay back? Dear reader, planning has the biggest return on investment of anything you've ever seen.

6

What If Something Goes Wrong?

MAKING THE PLAN BULLET-PROOF

By the time you get to here, you're nearly ready to go. You have a plan and this plan connects four things:

◆ What (the project is delivering)

◆ When (the project is delivering it)

◆ Work – the amount of work or effort involved in getting the project done.

◆ Quality – there's a whole bunch of jobs or tasks in the plan whose purpose is to ensure the quality of the finished product. (Typically, such things as reviews, testing, quality assurance, walkthroughs, signoffs and so on.)

But before you make any commitments, there's just one other thing you must do: you have to remember that the plan you have built is still just a prediction. As such, it is *incredibly fragile*. If you were to commit to this plan, then as soon as any tiny unexpected thing happens, you would start to drift from it.

So what you have to do is to take this incredibly fragile plan and toughen it up. Think of it as getting it ready to go out into the world. Right now, it's like a newborn – it couldn't survive by itself in the world. After you've toughened it up, it's going to be like a nineteen-year-old with attitude: it could go out into the world, bad and unexpected things might happen to it and it could survive those things.

The way to toughen the plan up is to put a safety margin into it. And the way to do this is with two techniques – a belt-and-braces approach. One of these two techniques is that you put contingency in the plan; the other is that you do risk management.

You know unexpected things will happen on your project. Most of them won't be good either! Therefore you need to introduce contingency into the plan to cover those things you know are inevitable.

Risk analysis then says something a little different; it says wouldn't it be nice if you could figure out where the hot spots on your project are likely to be – those places where you know you're going to have difficulty. Worse case scenario, you'll be aware of them. Maybe then you cannot just be aware of them, you can actually *do* something about them. Perhaps you can reduce the likelihood that they will happen, or reduce the effect if they do occur or eliminate them altogether. 'If you don't actively attack the risks on your project', the saying goes, 'then the risks will actively attack you'. So, let's do it to them then, before they do it to us!

CONTINGENCY

You could put contingency into your plan using any of the four factors we have already mentioned above but probably the easiest single way to do this is to add some extra time onto the end date.

This has loads of advantages – it is very visual, very easy to track against, very simple to spot drift and hugely effective as an early warning system.

So, for example, supposing your project was due to start on 2 January and your plan so far showed it ending on 10 August, then you could add, for example, three weeks (twenty-one days) to the end date and call it 31 August.

Ordinarily, that should be the end of it but often it isn't. Often, if bosses or stakeholders see contingency in a plan, they will take it out (or try to do so). If you feel that's going to happen to you and you wouldn't be able to stop them, then you need to hide the contingency so they can't find it. So, how would you hide the contingency in this case?

Easy! Instead of putting your contingency in one big three-week lump, as in our example, you could slice it up and put a little into each of the big phases where it would be a less juicy target.

If you felt that still wouldn't hide it sufficiently – because they would comb through the plan and take out all the occurrences of 'Contingency' – then you could call it something else instead of 'Contingency'. Here, it would be just the thing to use vague words and phrases – 'Finalize documentation', 'Housekeeping', 'Cleanup' or similar would work just fine.

If it's a very technical project, you could use technobabble. For example, 'Update object-oriented table vectors' or 'Feinblatt algorithm' – you get the idea.

RISK ANALYSIS

Here's how to do a risk analysis:

1. Identify – ideally with your team again – the risks to the project. Risks are the things that can cause the project to get into trouble.

2. For each risk, grade it in terms of the likelihood of it happening. Use a three-point scale – 3=high, 2=medium, 1=low.

3. For each risk, grade it in terms of, were it to happen, what would be its effect? Use the same three-point scale above.

4. Multiplying (2) by (3) gives you your exposure to that particular risk – the larger the number, the greater the risk.

5. For each risk of Exposure 6 or 9, identify what action(s) you can take to reduce that risk.

6. These actions are jobs and need to go into your plan.

Here's an example of what a risk analysis might look like on a product development project. The risks are explained in more detail below:

Risk	Likelihood (L)	Impact (I)	Exposure =L×I	Action(s)
1. The latent burnout kicks in	3	3	9	
2. Scope creep	1	3	3	
3. Poor or inadequate project management	1	1	1	

Risk	Likelihood (L)	Impact (I)	Exposure =L×I	Action(s)
4. Inadequate resources	3	3	9	
5. People leave	3	3	9	
6. Charlie leaves	3	3	9	
7. Estimates are wrong	2	3	6	
8. Project is technically infeasible	1	3	3	

1. In this example, your team has just come off a project where they were working burnout hours. You see this as a big risk and your exposure is very high here.

2. So-called 'scope creep', where the scope of the project increases. For example, Marketing asks for 'just one more feature' and Product Development agrees to slip it in. Or, more dangerously, Marketing people creep down to Product Development and ask individual engineers. And more dangerously still, some engineer suddenly thinks, 'This'd be really neat'.

3. After reading this book? Don't be ridiculous!

4. You don't get enough supply to match the demand. This one is your big fear (and the fear of many other project managers).

5. This is another of your big fears – people leave. To some extent maybe it's already covered by number 1 but you want it highlighted.

6. And this is your fourth big one: it all falls apart if Charlie, your key man, leaves. You're reasonably close to Charlie and you don't think he's job hunting at the moment but you never can tell.

7. Estimates are wrong – always a fear but once again, if you're doing as this book says, not very likely but even so, you rate it a pretty high Exposure.

8. The project turns out to be technically unfeasible. Low risk – you're not really blazing a technical trail here.

Next, you add in the risk reduction actions:

1. You're going to try and make this project a happy one. You want to run it without endless amounts of continuous overtime.

4. And you're going to do everything you can to prevent this happening.

5. You're going to get to HR open up a recruitment pipeline so that there are at least some résumés from likely candidates in the hopper. Maybe also some incentives for the team.

6. The incentives will be the key here.

7. You need to be on the lookout for the first sign of drift between what was estimated and what actually starts happening

Risk	Likelihood (L)	Impact (I)	Exposure =L×I	Action(s)
1. The latent burnout kicks in	3	3	9	Avoid long hours
2. Scope creep	1	3	3	
3. Poor or inadequate project management	1	1	1	
4. Inadequate resources	3	3	9	It won't happen
5. People leave	3	3	9	◆ HR to get in some résumés ◆ Possible incentives
6. Charlie leaves	3	3	9	Possible incentives
7. Estimates are wrong	2	3	6	Monitor estimated against actuals to ensure early warning
8. Project is technically infeasible	1	3	3	

GO DO IT!

Now go do both these things – add contingency and do a risk analysis – on your own project. Twenty minutes should be enough, half an hour tops.

PLANNING TIME TAKEN

So there we are – plan ready – in under two hours. For a small or even a medium-sized project, your plan will be complete. With a much bigger project you'll be a good way there. And, as we've said before, even if you haven't had enough time to finish it, you can go back to your stakeholders and explain what you've already learned. If they then ask for more information or a completed plan, you ask for more time.

And whether you go with what you've got or go back to do some more work, gather more information and complete the plan, you're now perilously close to the point where you're going to have to negotiate with your stakeholders.

That's where we go next.

7

Giving Them What They Want

THE PLAN SAYS WE'RE GOOD

Now that your plan is done, you're ready to go and deal with the constraints.

Of course the first possibility is that what the plan says is possible and what the constraints say is necessary are the same. In other words, the plan says the constraints are achievable. In that case you're all set; you're in business. You have a realistic plan, your stakeholders are happy and you're ready to roll. Kiss, kiss, hug hug, off you go! And there should be every likelihood, provided the plan is executed properly (as we'll discuss in the next chapter), that you should deliver the project successfully.

The only problem with this sweet little scenario is that it just doesn't happen all that often. And generally, what's more likely, is that what the plan says is possible and what the constraints say is necessary are not the same. Then what do you do?

THE PLAN SAYS WE'RE *NOT* GOOD

If the plan says the constraints are not achievable, is your only option then to say, 'Sure' and just suck it up?

No! That's the last thing on earth you're going to do.

The plan that you've built – the one that enabled you to diagnose whether or not the constraints were achievable – is also your tool for dealing with this situation. Here's what you do.

As we've seen, your plan involves four factors. Once again, these are:

◆ What (the project is delivering)

◆ When (the project is delivering it)

◆ Work – the amount of work or effort involved in getting the project done

◆ Quality – there's a whole bunch of jobs or tasks in the plan whose purpose is to ensure the quality of the finished product. (Typically, such things as reviews, testing, quality assurance, walkthroughs, signoffs and so on.)

The situation you now find yourself in is that you have a version of the plan that the stakeholders don't find acceptable. In other words, it's like you have a vanilla plan, but the stakeholders don't like vanilla.

But that's no problem, you can make other flavours. By varying the four parameters you can come up with other flavours of the plan that the stakeholders may like. And not only that, the stakeholders can ask about certain flavours – custom flavours, if you like – and you can see if you can make those flavours.

It's important, however, for everybody to realize that your plan (our ice cream machine!) is not infinitely variable. There are certain flavours that it may not be able to make. If that's the case then you need to tell that to the stakeholders and stop them choosing an impossible flavour.

Here's how you can vary the four parameters.

What

◆ You can 'de-scope' the project. That is, you can do less. You could categorize what the project is delivering into 'have to haves' and 'nice to haves', then maybe you just deliver the 'have to haves'.

◆ You could deliver the project incrementally – 'We can't give it all to you by the date you require [for example], but we could give you some and then a bit more and a bit more. Would that work for you?'

When

You can try to understand the significance of the constraints date we've been given. Some dates are inherently suspect:

◆ 24 December (or really, any date in the approximate range 20 December–3 January or so, i.e. the Christmas period). I accept that for some projects, e.g. the changeover to the Euro, the 31 December date had huge significance. But for many projects, these end-of-year dates are nothing more than the yearning of some tidy-minded person somewhere wanting the project to be over. (I accept also that this may be somewhat different in North America, where Christmas holidays are generally not so long.)

◆ Check what day of the week the constraints date falls on. If it's a Saturday or a Sunday, or a public holiday then, once again, it may not have any real significance. It often means that nobody has actually thought out why the end date is important. When you force them to do so it may buy you some extra time. (Once again, I accept that weekend dates can have a huge significance, e.g. they can be to do with taking live systems down and replacing or upgrading them. It's still worth asking, though.)

◆ 'Fluffy' dates – when stakeholders say something like 'end July' or 'early September'. It means they don't have a hard date in mind. If somebody said 'early September' to me, I would start the bidding at 30 October!

◆ In some countries, some months are holiday months, e.g. August in France or July in Sweden, so often – again, not always – a constraints date occurring in these months may not be a hard date, or there may be some 'give' in it.

◆ Finally, the constraints date may be to do with your stakeholders wanting to carve out some contingency for themselves. For instance, they need the thing done by say, 31 August, but they've told you 10 August. Thus, if you slip, they'll still have a good chance of being on time. So, in this example, 31 August may actually be the real constraints date.

Probing these things doesn't always help – but it certainly can't hurt. Don't automatically assume that every date you're given is a hard date: it may not be.

Work
You can look and see what the effect of adding more people to the project would be. However, you need to be a bit careful with this one. There's an effect known as Brooks' Law,[1] which says that, 'Adding people to a late project makes it later'. More generally, adding people to a project won't necessarily speed it up.

While this may sound counterintuitive, if you think about it then you can see why this would be true. Think of all the things that have to be done to bring new people onto a project. There is finding them, recruiting or assigning them, bringing them on board, finding places for them to work, tools for them to work with, bringing them up to speed, the time this takes away from existing team members. When you factor all this in, it's easy to see how adding people to a project could have:

◆ Little effect
◆ No effect
◆ And it might actually slow the whole thing down.

On the other hand, it may be possible to parachute in some specialists who'll be able to hit the ground running. In that case, you may indeed be able to, say, shorten the project and bring, say, a plan date closer to a constraints date.

I'm not saying don't use this one, just be careful of it. It could have unintended consequences.

Quality

Finally, maybe you can reduce the amount of testing or quality assurance (QA) you had planned to do, and still have something the stakeholders will be happy with. Or – more promising – can you get reviews and signoffs completed more quickly? Can people – especially stakeholders – turn things around quicker, get you decisions faster, so that you can gain some precious days and make the plan date and the constraints date converge? If the stakeholders are pushing you, push some of the responsibility back onto them and show that they too can make a contribution to the success of the project and to giving them what they want.

By varying some or all of these four parameters, in any combination, you can come up with alternative versions of the plan, and you should be able to convince the stakeholders that their best chance lies with one of these. Equally, you should be able to discourage stakeholders from choosing a course of action that your plan says cannot be achieved and is doomed to failure.

This is your first, most important and most promising strategy. It should be possible to solve all constraints-type problems in this way. If people are of goodwill and want the best for the project, then this is how these situations should always be handled. Stakeholders asking for impossible courses of action should be told politely but firmly that what they are asking for is not a runner – 'This dog won't hunt!' The plan and the facts in it – and *only* these – should be used as the basis for any discussion, negotiation and agreement. Anyone engaging in bullying, unreasonable behaviour or trying to pretend there isn't a problem ['So, we're all agreed then – the date's achievable?'] should be pulled back gently to the reality in the plan and told to consider the facts.

WHAT IF THAT DOESN'T WORK?

If the approach we've just described doesn't work with your stakeholders then you're going to need stronger medicine. You'll know if things are not working out because you'll end up dealing with situations or stakeholders where reason no longer prevails. You may hear things like this:

◆ 'Saying no is not an option', or

◆ 'I'm sorry – you just have to do it', or

◆ 'Sure, it's an aggressive schedule, but I'm sure you'll find a way', or

◆ 'The problem with you is that you're far too negative', or

◆ 'You're going to have to learn to be more flexible', or

◆ 'That's not the culture around here', or

◆ 'We need can-do people here', or

◆ 'Don't bring me problems, bring me solutions', or

◆ 'Is this plan based on a five-day week?', or

◆ 'If you don't do it, I'll find somebody who will'

◆ Or far worse things!

Sometimes – it must be said – this pressure to take on an impossible project may not come from external sources at all: you may generate it yourself. You may want to show that you're made of the right stuff, that you have what it takes. As a result, when somebody says, 'This is a very aggressive schedule', some macho thing within you takes over so you draw yourself up to your full height and say, 'This is the hour, cometh the man (or woman)!'

Whether internally or externally, if you find yourself under this pressure, what you *should* do is say 'no' – decline the impossible project.

If you say yes, let me tell you what's going to happen to you.

BECOMING A MAGICIAN

If you say 'yes' to an impossible project, then sometimes your efforts result in monumental disasters. But sometimes – incredibly – you manage to pull it off. You take something that everybody said was impossible and somehow you manage to get it done.

If you do this, if you manage to pull off an impossible mission, then you join a very select club that is called the Magicians' Club. Magicians do exactly as the name suggests: they do magic tricks, they take things which looked as though they couldn't be done and they make them happen.

And, in a sense, you can't say enough good things about Magicians. They provide an astonishing level of service – they do magic tricks, they take impossible things and they make them happen. Imagine you went to a job interview and the interviewer asked, 'What do you do?' and you replied, 'I do impossible missions.' They'd hand you the contract and say, 'How much do we have to pay you to come and do that for us?'

There are other good things that can be said about Magicians. It's true to say that not everybody in the company is a Magician; we'd all have to nod our heads on that one. And so, companies should love their Magicians – bring them flowers and champagne and presents on their birthday. Give them bonuses and stock options and salary raises and company cars and all the rest of it. Love them to death.

But there is a problem with being a Magician that we need to talk about: there is a dark secret at the heart of being a Magician. It's probably best illustrated by this graph.

On the horizontal axis is time; on the vertical one is how impossible the mission is. At the lower end of the scale, the mission is only mildly impossible. However, at the high end, everybody's completely lost the plot. So, as with all Magicians, your career starts out at the lower end of the scale: you begin by doing low-grade tricks.

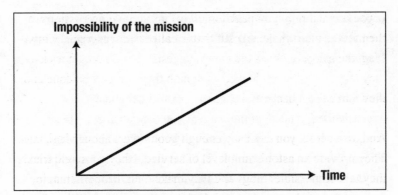

Figure 7.1: The problem with being a Magician

So, try and imagine now that you're in a theatre. In the front row, just beyond the footlights, you can see all of your stakeholders. There's your boss, your boss's boss, there's your team, your colleagues and co-workers, your customers and so on. Now, you walk on stage in your Magician's costume, and right before their eyes, you pull a rabbit from the hat. And the audience goes wild – they're applauding, cheering, whistling, stamping their feet. Your boss is nudging your boss's boss and saying, 'That's my Magician. I hired him/her. Isn't (s)he wonderful?' Your team are saying, 'S(he) led us to victory.' It's a sweet moment. If you've ever had one, and I'm sure you have, you'll know just how sweet it can be.

Now the next time you go on stage, a rabbit from the hat really isn't going to impress anybody. But that's okay. Encouraged by your success, you'll try a bigger animal. Little dogs to begin with – poodles and then bigger dogs. German Shepherds. And then a very big dog indeed: an Irish Wolfhound. And that probably does it with canines. So you move on to equines – mules, donkeys, ponies, racehorses, show jumpers. Then – relentlessly – giraffes, hippopotamuses, rhinoceros, elephants. If you stay at this long enough, eventually you'll pull the biggest mammal on Earth from the hat: the blue whale. All 200 tons of it, pulled – excruciatingly – from the hat.

And while most of the stakeholders are still delighted – overwhelmed, indeed, at the scale of your achievement – there are some who aren't quite so perky as they were when all this began. Your team, for example, is exhausted, having just endured another 'death march' project.[2] And for the first time, you notice some stakeholders to whom you hadn't really paid much attention before. In the second row are the husbands, wives, children, lovers, boyfriends, girlfriends, brothers, sisters, parents and pets – those people who love us and like to see us occasionally. They're not looking particularly thrilled as your Magician performances mean that you spend increasingly less time with them.

You would think that when you'd done the blue whale, you could stop. And you'd think that the company would put up a little plaque on your office door or cubicle wall. It would say, 'This is Charley's office. She pulled the blue whale from the hat. Tread softly as you walk by'. You would have a sort of honorary retirement, and people would come and gaze in at you as the person who had achieved so much.

Of course, nothing could be further from the truth. Once you've done the blue whale, then the stakeholders will just look for a more spectacular trick. Given that there are no bigger mammals to pull from hats, you turn your attention to sawing the lady in half. (I'm assuming you know this trick: there's a large rectangular box, a bit like a big coffin. A woman lies in it. Her head sticks out of a hole at one end and her feet stick out of two holes at the other. The magician takes a saw and saws the box down the centre. Then he separates the two pieces of the box. The woman's head and torso are in one section of the box and they appear to be separated from her legs and feet, which are in the other.)

So you start sawing ladies in half and the stakeholders are stunned. They thought they'd seen it all with mammals from hats, but this has brought your magicianship to a whole new level.

Now, one night you go out on stage, you put the lady in the box and you start the chainsaw. You saw down the centre of the box and fountains of blood come out everywhere. The trick goes horribly wrong. And it's a terrible moment; it's a terrible, *terrible* moment. It's terrible for all the stakeholders. It's particularly terrible for your team, who have worked so hard only to see the whole thing go horribly wrong. It's terrible for the stakeholders – they hadn't been expecting this. And sometimes the retribution can be terrible.

So, what happens to Magicians after that? Well, for a while they may stay in that organization; they may even continue to go on stage but when they do, the confidence of former times is replaced by terror. You don't know, the stakeholders don't know, the lady in the box doesn't know (!), what's going to happen when you start the chainsaw. Almost inevitably, the haggard, stumbling figure of the burned-out (for such they are) Magician moves on. They go to a new company or organization where their reputation does not precede them. And have they learned from this bitter experience?

Nope!

They start out low on the scale again, with low-grade tricks, pulling rabbits and other small creatures from hats. But it's only a matter of time before they replay the whole scenario we've already described and end up in the same place.

So, to use a popular word, the dark heart of being a Magician is that it is *unsustainable*. It may have some short-term benefits – to the team, your colleagues, your boss, your company, your customers. Long-term, it is of no benefit to anybody. All that happens is that you and the team work harder and harder, longer and longer hours, and you get closer and closer to the point where you're going to commit a monumental screw-up. Could anything be more unattractive?

That's what's going to happen to you if you continue to say 'yes' to impossible missions.

DESPERATE REMEDIES

If all of the preceding hasn't worked for you, here is a bunch of more desperate remedies that will also fix the problem; and by 'fix', I mean fix it to the satisfaction of all the stakeholders.

Before you read it, can I ask that you try again – *please* – to resolve the negotiation using the techniques already described. Only if these have proved completely impossible should you consider unwrapping what follows. What follows are four desperate remedies, four things you could try when all else has failed.

You could say 'yes'

In certain circumstances saying 'yes' might be a wise decision. This may sound as if I'm contradicting all my previous advice, but I'm not: there's a difference between saying 'yes' on a one-off basis and always doing so. You could possibly choose this tactic if the gap between what the plan says is possible and what the constraints says is necessary was not too great. Suppose you did cancel vacations, work weekends and late nights. If you factor all that additional effort into the plan, would that make things come right? (Notice again that you're using the plan to guide you.)

If the answer is no, then you need to look at one of the other three tactics which follow.

However, if the answer is yes, you then need to go and say to your team, 'What about it, team?' If they're not up for this, then you need to move on to one of the tactics that follow. And if they are, maybe you want to go back and say 'yes' to your stakeholders. But be conscious of everything we said about Magicians. If this project works out, what will your stakeholders expect after this?

But if this truly is a one-off, it may be that in these very specific circumstances:

◆ Very definitely a one-off project, and

◆ The gap between the plan and constraints is bridgeable according to the plan, and

◆ Your team is up for it

then saying 'yes' may constitute a wise decision. However, this is playing with fire since you are taking a drug that can be very hard to get off after you've tasted it once.

You could say 'no'
It may be that everyone has completely lost the plot, i.e. the gap between what the plan says is possible and what the constraints says is necessary is so great that it could never be bridged.

In that case, you want to get a million miles away from the project because when the bomb goes off here, the mess is going to be appalling. Document your reasons for passing on the project. You can add to your document your prediction of what you believe is going to happen (based on the plan), i.e. the mess that will be created if the plan is committed to in its current form.

Finally, if you really want to rub it in, use your plan to say here's how that mess will have to be sorted out when the time comes. All of this should give your stakeholders major cause for thought. In my experience, it has often – though not always – been enough to bring stakeholders around to your point of view.

For you, in these circumstances, saying 'no' might constitute a wise decision.

You could play the big change game
In construction, where the lowest bidder often gets the job, they do this all the time – and highly successfully.

Let's say your plan says that the project is going to cost €/$/£ 500K and the stakeholders say you have to do it for €/$/£ 350K, an impossible mission.

You say, 'Sure, I'll take it for 350.'

Now every time the stakeholders make the teensiest change to what they asked for, you say, 'Hey, that's a change!' In addition, you use slips on the stakeholder side to mask any slips on your side.

It might well be that in using this tactic you take an impossible project and manage your way to making it possible. So, is this a wise decision? Could hardly be wiser! People in construction make big profits using this technique.

You could accept the project but not accept the constraints

A neat trick and here's how it works. Let's say you have a project where the constraints date is 6 September but the plan says 29 November – an impossible mission.

Now, it's important to realize that you have one weakness in all of this – a weakness upon which the stakeholders may pounce. 'Ah-ha,' they may say, 'your plan is a prediction and so it might all be wrong! You could have over-estimated everything and this project could be very do-able.'

'It *could* be,' you agree reasonably. 'I could have under-estimated everything too, of course, so that the situation could be far worse than I've said here. But here's what I'm prepared to do: I'll give it a try and here's what I guarantee. I don't believe 6 September is possible so I can't guarantee that. I *can* guarantee 29 November. But what I'll also do for you is that every week I'll tell you how we're doing.'

The stakeholders will always accept this. What they've heard is the sound of you getting into your Magician's costume. And what they believe you said was that you would give the project a try – in other words, you're going to have a crack at 6 September.

Now, that is not what you said so you need to start reminding them. The first week of the project you issue a status report that says:

Here's what you asked for: 6 September

Here's what we're committed to: 29 November

Here's what our plan is saying today: 29 November [It'd be a pretty bad plan if you couldn't keep it on target for the first week!]

You continue to do this every week. During this time your stakeholders will go through a period of denial where they're not listening to what you're saying so as well as writing the status report, you need to be bending their ear – we're probably talking primarily about your boss here – and saying, 'What are *you* going to do about this 6 September/29 November problem?' The 'you' is a very important word here. Remember, it's *their* problem, not yours. You never committed to 6 September, they did.

You keep doing this until they hear you. Then they may go into a period of irrational behaviour where they start using a lot of those unpleasant phrases that we saw earlier. However, you just keep beaming out the same message:

Here's what you asked for: 6 September

Here's what we're committed to: 29 November

Here's what our plan is saying today: We'd like to think it'd be on or before 29 November!

Finally, if you just stick to your guns and keep beaming out the status reports, eventually they will pass into the third phase where they wake up and smell the coffee and start to deal with *their* (not your) 6 September/29 November issue.

It's worth saying yet again, I think, that this tactic prolongs a negotiation that really should have been resolved as described at the beginning of this chapter but needs must. This tactic will give you a wise decision – especially if you have one or a group of extremely volatile, disagreeable (maybe even disturbed) stakeholders.

GO DO IT!

Now go do what we described here on some project that you are asked to do.

If you win the negotiation, great, but if you lose it, don't despair. It means you gave up; that you stopped believing in your plan. So replay the negotiation in your head. Identify the point at which you gave up. The next negotiation, take it a bit further. Don't give up so easily, eventually you will get one over the line.

This first one will be the hardest, it will get easier after that.

What will happen eventually is that you will wean yourself off behaving like a Magician and instead only make commitments that you can deliver on. This is what stakeholders want. They have no right to expect miracles and if they've come to expect them, it's only because you've been giving them miracles.

Give it up! Otherwise sooner or later it's going to end in tears.

Give them predictability. If you can do that, you'll be an extraordinary employee and a great team player indeed.

PLANNING TIME TAKEN

This negotiation may only take you a few minutes. However, it could end up saving you weeks, months, possibly even years of grief.

8

Getting It Done

To get the project done, you need to:

◆ Get the jobs done
◆ Track progress on the plan
◆ Report the status to the stakeholders
◆ And, finally, do a post-mortem at the end.

GETTING THE JOBS DONE

This is not a book about how to manage, motivate and get the best out of people. There are such books – and courses you can attend and degrees you can do and material on the Internet. Whole rainforests have been levelled to write books, learned articles, treatises and theses on the subject. If you're interested you should go find some of them. (*Shackleton's Way: Leadership Lessons from the Great Antarctic Explorer*[3] is one of my favourites.)

But here, I just want to make one key point on the subject – a point that while very obvious once it's pointed out, was a huge eye-opener for me in my management career.

It is that one size doesn't fit everybody.

To explain.

It's true to say that each of us, depending on our personality, has what might be called our 'natural' management style. Some people are very hands-off. 'There's no point in having a dog,' the saying goes, 'and barking yourself'. In other words, if somebody has a job to do, let them get on with it and trust they will do it properly. Then, on the other end of the spectrum, there are those who are very hands-on. Only by micromanaging everything do they feel that they're in control and can be sure that things are on track. Control freaks, in other words.

So, which is right? The former sounds like a nice regime to work under – the person being managed can use his/her own initiative and creativity – but it sounds like things could go a long way wrong here before they were spotted. The latter regime sounds a lot more safe and secure, but it also sounds like it could be a giant pain to work under (or indeed to have to apply) such a regime.

The answer, of course, is that one size doesn't fit everybody and that no matter what your personality causes you to do 'naturally', you're going to have to be a bit more versatile when it comes to managing people.

◆ Where the evidence is that when you give them a job, it gets done, then leave them alone and let them get on with it. This is true even if your natural style is to micromanage; this will only be counterproductive here. 'If it ain't broke don't fix it', the saying goes – and it isn't broke here. And the key, of course, is evidence – the facts. This isn't about whether you like somebody or think they're smelly or would loan them twenty quid, it's all based on facts. When you give them a job, it gets done. Or not.

◆ Where:

◆ Somebody doesn't report to you – somebody in another group or department or organization; or

◆ Is inexperienced; or

◆ You're unsure about their ability,

then you need to stay on their case a bit (or a lot) more. This is where micromanagement is good and hands-off would be very bad – again, irrespective of what your personality drives you to do.

TRACKING THE PROJECT

'Tracking the plan' means two things. It means (a) ensuring that what the plan says should be happening is happening; and (b) that what happens on the project is reflected in the plan.

Here's how to do that:

1. Look down the plan from top to bottom and identify any task that requires some action by you today.

2. Add these actions to your to-do list for today.

3. Complete these actions.

4. For each task completed, record the results (actual work, actual duration) in the plan. (Put two extra columns in your plan.)

5. For each unexpected event that occurs on the project, determine whether or not it's a big change, i.e. whether it falls into any of the following three categories:

◆ An assumption turns out to be false

◆ Changes to the scope of the project, i.e.increases in demand –
   more features, extra deliverables, that sort of thing

◆ Changes to the resourcing, i.e. (usually) reductions in the
   supply – people leave or you lose them to another project.

6. If the unexpected event is any of these three, then you need to
   revise the plan, show it to the stakeholders and agree this new
   plan with them just as you did in Chapter 7 (page 55). Thus, for
   example, if the stakeholders increase the scope of the project and
   take some of your people for a more sexy project, then you need
   to show that yes, for sure, they can do that – it's their right – but
   then they must accept the consequences that you're showing
   them in this revised plan.

7. If the unexpected event is not any of these three, then you either
   need to use the contingency to deal with it or work some extra
   time to deal with the unexpected event. A word of caution too
   on contingency: even if you have contingency, you might choose
   to work extra time. Why? Well, you don't want to blow your
   contingency early in the project – you may well need it at the
   end. You don't want to be going into the later stages of your
   project with your contingency tank empty.

8. Finally, check to see whether the delivery date of the project (and
   the budget and the person-days, if you were tracking those) has
   changed. If they haven't then the project is on target. And if they
   have improved, say nothing. If they have disimproved then this
   is a warning sign. A single disimprovement by itself may not be
   a problem, since the slip could be corrected but if, every time

you run the routine we've decribed here, the disimprovement is getting worse, then this is a sign that you're in trouble and you're going to have to tell this to the stakeholders. (We cover communicating bad news to the stakeholders in the next section.)

REPORTING THE STATUS

We have stressed already just how important it is to set the expectations of the stakeholders. Setting them correctly at the beginning of the project is obviously crucial to its success – it would be hard to imagine anything more crucial. As the project unfolds, however, it is your job to ensure that the expectations continue to be managed. For any kind of decent-sized project, a weekly status report is the way to do that.

Many status reports, either intentionally or otherwise, do not make the status of the project particularly clear: obfuscation is the order of the day. There are rambling accounts of all kinds of activity on the project, and a feeling that though things are running pretty close to the wind, we'll be alright on the night. Status reports have a lot in common with fairy stories – two things notably. One is that almost all status reports have a happy ending. There is a feeling that despite all our trials and tribulations things are going to turn out okay. The other similarity is that lots of the status reports I've seen in my time *are* fairy stories, i.e. the things described in them never happened or happened only in the author's mind.

Most project managers aren't very good at status reporting. That previous sentence is probably one of the understatements of all time. Usually the problem is one of the following three things:

◆ The project manager doesn't actually know the status of the project. (If (s)he didn't have a properly constructed plan then a real, true status is impossible to establish.)

◆ (S)he knows but (s)he'd much rather (s)he didn't know.

◆ (S)he knows, (s)he'd much rather (s)he didn't know and (s)he'll be damned if (s)he's going to tell anybody until (s)he really, *really* has to. (And by then, (s)he may have gotten a lucky break on the project – or somebody may have offered him/her a new job!)

What you need to do then is to tell the stakeholders the status in such a way that the message is not garbled, misunderstood, hidden or reversed. Also, we don't want to be writing *War and Peace* here, we want to get this done as quickly as possible. Here's how to do that: do it in three layers.

Layer 1
Quite simply, is the project on target or not? Almost always, we are interested in the delivery date – and we might also want to know whether the budget and/or person-days were on target.

Layer 2
Here, we need to explain how we got to be where we are. We need to give a change history – again of the delivery date (and of the budget and person-days, if you were tracking those). Here's an example of a change history.

Date of change	Reason for change	General availability date
	Original dates	1 September 2014
9 May 2014	Scope of the project increased by the stakeholders	23 January 2014
27 May 2014	Lost two of the team to another project	31 January 2014
2 July 2014	Had assumed four rounds of testing. Turned out to be seven	5 February 2014
14 October 2014	Estimates for integration were too low	10 February 2014

Why write change histories? Well, if you don't write them, what happens? In this example here's what happens. Some time after 1 September 2014, some genius looks at this project and says, 'What's going on here? This project was meant to finish on 1 September but it's still running.' What do they do next? Next, they send out a bullet to all and sundry saying, 'What's going on here? Who's responsible for this slip?' (Note that at this stage this can only be a 'slip'. The notion there might have been any other reason – for example, requests for changes by the stakeholders or people denuding your project of resources – are well and truly forgotten.)

So, what happens then? What happens then is that everybody starts writing change histories showing how they're not guilty of causing the 'slip'. Then you get into conversations like, 'Do you not remember that meeting where you said . . . ?' 'No,' is usually the innocent answer. 'But I sent you an email where I said and you agreed . . .' 'No, I never got that email.' And then you're well and truly in trouble.

By writing change histories you – and *only* you – write the history of the project, the here's-how-we-got-to-be-where-we-are-now.

Layer 3

Level 3 is the everything-and-the-kitchen-sink level. Here, you can give them the current version of the plan, the current risk analysis and anything else that you fancy. If you want to write 'Tasks Completed Last Week/Tasks Planned for Next Week' you can do that. And if you want to mention everybody on the team in dispatches and say who's working on what, you can do that. All of this is good stuff but it's nowhere near as important as what we put into levels 1 and 2.

DOING A POST-MORTEM

Post-mortems tend not to get done very often, which is a great pity. The result is that often we go on to repeat the same mistakes over and over again.

Usually, when they are done, they contain a mine of useful information. In particular, they contain a whole bunch of recommendations – things that should be done to improve the way projects are done. The problem then, of course, is that nobody has time to carry out these recommendations – everybody is already pushing on to the next great thing.

So there's a lot to be said then for a light post-mortem – one that could be done quickly and might also result in some improvements. So here's a light post-mortem. Three things:

1. The project as it actually panned out – your plan as it eventually finished. If you updated the plan as we described above, this

will be in your hand at the end. You won't have to do any extra work to get it. This stuff will be so invaluable when you come to plan your next project. It will help to make your estimating even more accurate. If you're doing a similar project, you will have a template for how to do it. If your next project is very dissimilar, almost certainly there will be things you can learn from the completed project that you can carry over to the next one.

2. What's one thing we did well on this project? Some technique you used or template you developed or tool you used, or app you found or piece of information you discovered that really made a difference. Be sure to do/use this thing again. But also, share it around. Tell all your colleagues – 'We found this useful, you might too.'

3. And then – similarly, what's one thing you did badly on this project? Something that, if you could rewind the clock, you would do differently? This caused us problems, it messed us around, had we known this, we would have gone a different way. Be sure *not* to do this thing again. But also, share it around. Tell all your colleagues. This is harder to do but if you could, it might stop other people falling into the trap you fell into.

GO DO IT!

Now go do what we've described here on some project you're running.

PLANNING TIME TAKEN

You won't find a more efficient way to get your project done than the method I've described here. And I say this, having spent years trying to whittle it down to this.

Part 2

Planning for your Organization

9

Why Fate Runs Most Organizations

If you run an organization – a group/department/division/company – then planning can make a profound change to the way you work and bring unbelievable benefits. First, let's look at the way most organizations run. If you read this chapter and find nothing that resonates with you, then you must be already doing what we're about to describe in this, the second part of the book.

Almost all organizations, no matter what sector or business they are in, operate in broadly the same way. In a typical organization this is what happens. At the beginning of the year, the owners or shareholders or board decide that they want to do 'more' business as usual. They say they want to capture X per cent more customers or market share, increase revenue by Y or profit by Z, sell such and such a per cent more widgets and so on. Also, they want to do some brand-new things – new products, services, initiatives, take new directions.

The management team takes this mission and launches a bunch of projects designed to make sure that both of these major thrusts (business as usual and new initiatives) are realized. They often use phrases similar to those we already saw in the 'What If That Doesn't Work?' section of Chapter 7 (page 60). While some of these phrases may sound quite different from each other, in fact they all have common undertones. These undertones are:

◆ What we're being asked to do is really tough.

◆ But it's certainly doable.

◆ And we know you're the man/woman for the job.

◆ And if you say you can't do it, you're being disloyal in some way.

◆ Besides, planning is for wimps – the way to get this done is just to go in and do it.

Everybody in the organization now has (a) maybe a day job and (b) almost certainly, a project-related workload. Most management teams expect everybody to undertake such a workload. For this reason planning becomes somewhat secondary. Indeed planning can come to be viewed as something of a problem. After all, we don't want plans showing us that the things we are trying to do are impossible, now do we?

Because plans are non-existent or inadequate, there is no real measure of whether there are enough people to do all the work. The suspicion (or it could be much stronger than that) is that there aren't. But it doesn't matter because somehow, the view is we'll find a way. In reality, that 'somehow' is generally pretty obvious and well known to everybody. If there aren't enough people to do all the work, then the existing ones can just work harder. And this is exactly what happens – the troops begin to work harder and harder, longer and longer hours – ten to sixteen hours a day over sustained periods of time.

Despite this, something – either a project or some business-as-usual thing – starts to drift. (This is inevitable if there aren't enough people to do all the work.) Eventually – it's usually as late as possible because nobody wants to be seen to be the bearer of bad news – somebody realizes that there's a problem.

When this happens there's a bit of a stink. Some senior manager or customer begins to jump up and down about 'their' thing. If they shout loud enough people are switched onto that thing and the thing that lost the people is told to work even harder. You then get the phenomenon known as 'constantly changing priorities'.

Those people *do* work harder – but it doesn't make any difference. That or some other thing now starts to drift, despite the long hours being worked. And the thing to which people were moved doesn't necessarily speed up. There are learning curves and people need to come up to speed and they make mistakes that those who were already familiar with the thing had stopped making ages ago.

Life carries on like this until management realizes that something else is drifting. The same events occur – a stink, jumping up and down, people being moved from one thing to another, the progress on more and more things not being what was expected. And so the year unfolds. By now firefighting has become standard operating procedure.

Eventually the end of the year comes round. Some things have been done, many haven't. Many have come in late and/or over-budget. Right up to the last minute it's not been 100 per cent clear which things – out of all the things we set out to do at the beginning of the year – are going to end up being done and which will be left undone. Projects have been completed with huge effort and overtime. Some projects have not been completed at all or have gone badly astray. There is a sense that there has been a lot of wasted time, effort, resources and money; there is also a permanent backlog, which never seems to get cleared.

As for the people – well – some people are burnt out and leave. The pressure and stress are so severe that they may have affected people's health. Work/life balance feels like a thing of the past. (People's feelings about work may range from 'don't particularly enjoy working here' through to 'dread going to work in the morning'). At best, everybody thinks it's been a tough year and that they worked really hard. There is a sense of having triumphed in the face of adversity. We sure earned our salaries and bonuses this year, we think. Yep – we did one hell of a job!

And there is a feeling that while the way we do things at the moment may not be perfect, it's the best way there is – that this is just 'the culture of the organization'.

You may think that you – the management – are running the organization but are you really? Were the things that got done the ones that mattered most? Maybe . . . but maybe not. In the end there was no conscious decision making about this. It wasn't really the management that decided; it was decided more by the series of events that unfolded.

In other words, Fate/luck/chance decided.

If any of this sounds familiar, if you saw any of these symptoms in your organization, then planning can fix all of that. And if you'd like to take back your organization from Fate, the remainder of Part 2 of this book shows you how to do that in six easy steps.

10

Step 1 – Just How Good Are You?

It's always good to see how you're already doing before you start to improve something so that's what you're going to do first. This will enable you to see:

◆ How much Fate *does* actually control your organization and

◆ How far you've come when you've gone through the remaining steps in this process.

To see how you're already doing, there are four things you must do:

1. Decide what period of time you want to look at.

2. Make a list of all the projects you are doing or plan to do over that period.

3. Figure out the status of each project. This will use a scheme that is described below.

4. Calculate what is called the Organizational Performance Indicator (OPI).

This chapter tells you what to do and gives you an example. You can use it as a template for your own work.

(1) DECIDE WHAT PERIOD OF TIME YOU WANT TO LOOK AT

What you are going to do in the next few chapters will fundamentally change the way you run your organization. So, in terms of its importance and its effect on the organization, it is probably comparable to when you do your strategic planning for the year. For that reason then, it probably makes sense to use the same kind of period of time that you would use if you were doing strategic planning. Thus – and this is just a suggestion – if you were doing this work in January through May of a particular year, you might want to look at the period from where you are now to the end of that year. If you were doing this work in June through December, you might want to consider looking at the rest of that year and the following year.

(2) MAKE A LIST OF ALL OF THE PROJECTS

You need to identify all of the projects you are doing or plan to do over that period. This will include three types of project:

◆ Known and committed projects: Projects that you know about and to which the organization is committed.

◆ 'I didn't know we were doing that' projects: Projects that somehow came into life and are currently being worked on. The reason why they are in existence may not be 100 per cent clear, nor may it be clear who authorized them or how they came to life. But somewhere along the way, somebody committed something to somebody so that now you have to take this into account.

◆ Future projects: You're going to have to make some attempt to predict what projects you might have to do over the period of time in question. The things you learned about estimating in Chapter 4 (*see also* page 25) will enable you to do this.

Now obviously for a very large organization there could be hundreds and hundreds of projects. So if this is your first time trying all of this, you may want to reduce the size of the organization you are looking at, e.g. rather than looking at a whole company you may want to look at just one division or group or section.

Known and committed projects

This should be the easiest part of the procedure. You need to make a list of all the projects that the organization is involved in and committed to at the moment. Maybe the list already exists and gets reported on every week. Or perhaps there's no list but everybody knows (or thinks they do!). Or maybe you're not 100 per cent sure. In that case, get the people together who do know and make the list. You just want a list at this stage. No calculations or anything else – just the names of the projects.

'I didn't know we were doing that' projects

Such projects may well not appear on any list – at least not any central, consolidated, organization-wide one. These are the projects that just somehow got started – maybe nobody's 100 per cent sure exactly how. Perhaps the boss (or somebody else) just came in one day and said, 'Forget everything else, I've got a really great idea' or 'Maybe we could just investigate this' or 'Don't spend too much time on this, but . . .'. Or maybe there's some maverick in the organization somewhere responsible for it. In a sense it doesn't matter – at least, for now it doesn't. For now what matters is that somebody has committed something to somebody. (If that second somebody is one of your organization's customers, then that makes the commitment especially serious.) For now, though, you just need to get its name onto your list.

Future projects

In general you won't know for sure everything you're going to do in the future. Some projects will depend on whether you win certain business or get certain customer orders. Whether you go ahead with some projects or not will depend on the business climate at the time. You can only make some kind of prediction or best guess now. So what you're going to do is to do exactly that – make a prediction. In other words, an estimate, as described in Chapter 4 (*see also* page 25). To do this you're going to make some assumptions – in other words, your best guess – about which projects are going to happen over the period that you're looking at.

(3) FIGURE OUT THE STATUS OF EACH PROJECT

Next, you need to identify the status of each project. For now, you will do that with what we will call a 'soft audit'. Later on we will look at the more definitive way to do it.

A soft audit is the simplest, quickest and least-threatening (to the person whose project is being audited) way to assess the health of a project. All you do is ask the project manager what the status is and whatever s(he) says you take as gospel. Each project is then given one of the following four statuses:

◆ Green (which gets score of 5)   The project has a written plan and is a running to plan

◆ Amber (score of 3)   The project has a written plan but has run into some problems. The project manager

is addressing them and expects to bring
the project back to green.

◆ Blue (scores 0)   The project has no written plan.

◆ Red (scores −1)   Whether or not the project had a written
plan, it is now out of control.

So, in detail then:

1. Does the project have a written plan? (You don't even have to ask
   to see it.) If they say yes, then go to question 2. Otherwise this is
   a Blue (0).

2. Is the project on target? If the Project Manager says yes, then
   you just take his/her word for it. The project is Green (5). If the
   answer is no, go to question 3.

3. How much is the project off-target? If the answer is to the effect
   of 'a little but we can/are taking steps to rectify it', then this is an
   Amber (3). If the answer is to the effect of 'very much', then this
   is a Red (−1).

Now enter these scores beside your list of projects.

It's perhaps worth saying at this point that in reality things rarely
turn out as rosily as this picture generally shows:

Often Greens (On target) are not really. The plan was never accurate
in the first place or is out of date, or is not being tracked properly.
Or even all three.

◆ Ambers (Some problems) are really Reds. The some-problems-
  which-could-be-fixed are actually huge problems which are

going to require a fundamental re-planning of the project and a new agreement with the stakeholders.

◆ Greens and Ambers are often Blues. The plan – such as it is – isn't actually worth the paper it's written on.

However, you don't need to worry about this for the moment – you'll deal with all of that in due course. What you *do* need to start thinking about, though, is that any projects which are either Blue (No written plan) or Red (Out of control) should be considered as being 'At Risk'.

(4) CALCULATE THE ORGANIZATIONAL PERFORMANCE INDICATOR (OPI)

You can think of the OPI as a description of the organization. It is a description not in terms of its mission statement or its balance sheet, or its strategic plan or its business plan, or its organizational chart or the market sectors it services, or indeed any of the million-and-one other ways you could describe an organization. Rather, the organization is defined in terms of the projects it is running. In other words, we want to define the organization to be the sum of its projects.

To calculate the OPI, add up the individual scores of all the projects and divide the result by the total number of projects. The resulting number is a number between −1 and 5. The closer to −1 you are, the worse the shape in which your projects – and hence your organization – are. And the closer you are to 5, the better their shape. A score of 5 would mean that all your projects had been properly planned and were also running to plan. (Not an impossible idea, in case you were thinking otherwise!)

You'll see below that the OPI and associated project status chart give you – at a glance – a lot of incredibly useful information.

EXAMPLE – THE ACME COMPANY

To make this method as real as possible to you, and also to provide you with templates upon which you can base your own work, here's an example. This example concerns a (hypothetical) organization that develops technology products (we don't need to be any more precise than that). The company is called The Acme Company and employs just under forty people but plans to grow to nearly fifty within the next eighteen months (I have chosen an organization of this size only to keep the worked example to manageable proportions. At the end of each chapter I will mention briefly how this example could be scaled up or down).

Basically, the organization has a side that brings in business (Sales & Marketing) and a side that delivers the business (Product Development). This is what the organization is like in terms of numbers of people:

CEO, Finance, HR and admin staff	5
Sales & Marketing	6
Product Development	23
Product Support	3
Total	37

Figure 10.1: The Acme Company – Staffing

There is a CEO, a Finance person, a HR person and two admin staff. In Sales & Marketing, there is a Head of Sales, three salespeople, a Marketing person and an admin person. In Product Development, there is a Head of Product Development, three Team

Leaders/Section Managers and nineteen Development Engineers. Product Support, which looks after customers, takes support calls, does installation and training, consists of three people.

The Acme Company – 'Acme', for short – has been in business for about five years and has clients in several countries. It went through a couple of loss-making years as it was starting up, but for the last three years has made a profit. This profit has been reinvested in the company to continue its growth. It makes standard products and also does 'specials' – custom versions of its products for certain customers.

There are some problems in the organization. Sales & Marketing, which feels it's pretty good at what it does, has brought in lots of business. However, it constantly complains that Product Development essentially can't keep pace with them. Sales & Marketing brings the business in; Product Development makes commitments but then, rarely if ever, delivers on those commitments. Often too, if it does deliver on commitments, it is only after major heroics of working nights and weekends, with Sales & Marketing not knowing, right up to the last minute, whether or not the customer is going to get what was promised.

Product Development also feels it's pretty good at what it does. After all, they're the people who manage to pull off the impossible missions that Sales & Marketing keep handing them. Apart from the problem of impossible missions, Product Development constantly accuses Sales & Marketing of 'changing their minds all the time'. Sales & Marketing takes a different view: it sees it as 'doing whatever is necessary to win the business and keep the customer happy'.

Everybody's working long hours. Product Development is doing so for the reasons just cited. Sales & Marketing is doing so because it's hungry for business but also because its customer base is worldwide so Sales & Marketing people spend a lot of time on the road. It's always been like this in Acme, right from the start. During its first three or four years everybody was prepared to work the long hours on the basis that they were in start-up mode, and (as they saw it), that's just the way things are in a start-up. But now, as the company enters its sixth year of trading, people's enthusiasm and resilience are flagging a bit – they're wondering if it's always going to be like this.

Unfortunately, it's no longer the nineties when, if people felt like this, they could just walk down the street and get another job on a higher salary. The Recession has come and so, if anybody complains, it is hinted (or they are told straight out) that they're lucky to have a job. People kind of know this anyway, but it doesn't help to be told. In short, morale isn't what it used to be.

The CEO is an enlightened man and has been wondering for some time if there is a better way. He's bought the book you're holding in your hand and he's going to give it a shot.

EXAMPLE – STEP 1: MEASURE WHERE YOU ARE

(1) Decide what period of time you want to look at

It is 1 July as the CEO decides to try this out. Given that, with summer holidays and everything, July and August are a bit of a washout and after that there are only four months in the year (September to December), he decides to look at a period from now until the end of the following year. In total then, he is going to look at a period of eighteen months, 1 July of this year through to 31 December of next year. (As we said earlier, the choice is completely arbitrary.)

(2) Make a list of all of the projects

The CEO gets a status report every week from the Head of Product Development, which lists all of the projects and says what their status is. He uses this as a starting point, but then he checks with the Head of Sales & Marketing to find out whether this is the definitive list. He shows the Head of Sales & Marketing the list and essentially asks him, 'Can you think of any other project or product that is not on here that has been promised to customers in some way, shape or form?'

'Nope, that looks like it,' says the Head of Sales & Marketing.

Then, after a pause, he adds, 'Except for the so-and-so. I don't see that on there. And, of course, customer X is looking for the what's-its-name – we said we would do that for them. And I don't know if, when it says Product Y on that list, they mean the three different variants of Product Y. You should maybe check that.'

Just to be doubly on the safe side, the CEO suggests they call in the three sales people to see if they have any more things like this. Eventually, the meeting ends up being with the entire Sales & Marketing department and another couple of projects emerge from discussions.

Chastened, and a bit alarmed, the CEO has a similar conversation with the Product Development side of the house. One or two other so-called 'internal projects' emerge. In addition, the CEO makes a few decisions about things that should also be on the list. They are:

◆ All of these projects should be being properly project managed. He's not sure whether or not they are, but he knows (from Chapter 5, page 44) that each of the projects is going to require an additional 10 per cent of its total effort for project management. The CEO wants to make sure that's factored in so he's going to separate it out as a separate line item.

◆ He's also going to put in a line item called 'Product Support'. This is so that the three people who provide that will also be included in his calculations.

◆ Because the area of technology in which the company finds itself is so fast-changing, the CEO knows they will have to spend some of their time looking at new products and technologies so he's going to have a line item called 'New technologies'.

◆ He's also going to include a line item called 'Quality system'. The company is installing a new quality system and he reckons over the eighteen-month period he's looking at some proportion of people's time will go into that. He needs to allow for this.

◆ Also, he's going to include a line item called 'Training'. In general, the people he has hired are very new/young/ inexperienced. In addition, both the area of technology that the company is in and the development tools that the company uses are very new and fast-changing. Previously, working with the HR person, he has worked out that – to stay current and work effectively – his Product Development people each need about seven days' training a year. That's going to come to ten days over eighteen months.

◆ Next, he is going to include a line item called 'Contingency'. Is it likely that nothing will change in this industry or in this particular company over the next eighteen months? Come off it! Of course things will change. Naturally, unexpected things will occur. He needs to have something in reserve to cover this. Moreover, he has to make some assumptions about the additional projects that they will have to do over the next eighteen months. He does so as follows.

◆ Sales have about a 50 per cent hit rate. In other words, taking everything into account, they tend to win about half the business they bid for. So, the CEO has another conversation with the Head of Sales & Marketing about what proposals they have out, or are likely to put out, over the next eighteen months. He takes 50 per cent of this and that gives him a couple more projects for his list.

◆ Finally, he gazes into his CEO's crystal ball and just tries to imagine what else could occur over the next eighteen months that might cause more projects to go on the list.

So, having done all this work, here's what his list ends up looking like (Figure 10.2).

(3) Figure out the status of each project

The CEO then assesses the status of each project. He does this not by reading it from the status report but rather by going and asking each project manager. After asking them the three questions given earlier in this chapter (*see also* page 93), he marks the projects accordingly. What he finds is here (Figure 10.3).

	THE ACME COMPANY – PROJECT LIST		
1	**3041**		
	3041		
2		For Sweden	
3		For France	
4		For Spain	
5	**USB Widget**		
	3141 New architecture		
6		Sweden	
7		France	
8		Spain	
	Stand-alone gizmo		
9		Sweden	
10		France	
11		Spain	
	System-wide device		
12		Sweden	
13		France	
14		Spain	
	NPK 1622		
15		Sweden	
16		France	
17		Spain	
18	**Divergent NPK**		
	CEF	Variant 1	
19		Variant 2	
20			
	Product Support		
21		Existing products	
22		New products	
23	**Other variants**		
24	**New technologies**		
25	**Quality system**		
26	**Training**		
27	**Contingency**		
28	**Project management**		

Figure 10.2: Acme's initial project list

	THE ACME COMPANY – PROJECT LIST				Red/Amber/
				STATUS	**Green/Blue**
1	**3041**			On target	5
	3041				
2		For Sweden		No written plan	0
3		For France		Some problems	3
4		For Spain		On target	5
5	**USB Widget**			On target	5
	3141 New architecture				
6		Sweden		On target	5
7		France		On target	5
8		Spain		On target	5
	Stand-alone gizmo				
9		Sweden		On target	5
10		France		On target	5
11		Spain		On target	5
	System-wide device				
12		Sweden		Out of control	-1
13		France		Out of control	-1
14		Spain		Some problems	3
	NPK 1622				
15		Sweden		Out of control	-1
16		France		On target	5
17		Spain		Some problems	3
18	**Divergent NPK**			On target	5
	CEF	Variant 1			
19		Variant 2		Out of control	-1
20				On target	5
	Product Support			Some problems	3
21		Existing products			
22		New products		Some problems	3
23	**Other variants**			Some problems	3
24	**New technologies**			No written plan	0
25	**Quality system**			On target	5
26	**Training**			On target	5
27	**Contingency**			Out of control	-1
28	**Project management**			Out of control	-1
				Total of scores	82
				OPI	2.93
	Green (5) = On Track			14	
	Amber (3) = Warning! Some problems			6	
	Blue (0) No Plan Exists			2	
	Red (-1) = Runaway Project			6	
	Status unknown				
	TOTAL NUMBER OF PROJECTS			28	
	TOTAL AT RISK (RED or BLUE)			8	

Figure 10.3: Acme's initial project status

For the regular projects – numbers 1–21 – the CEO gets the status exactly as described above. For the others he has to interpret the guidelines a bit and this is how he chooses to do that:

◆ The Product Support people report – as they always do – that they have too few people for all of the support calls and other work they must do. The CEO chooses to rate this Amber on the basis that he wants to check at some stage the supply-demand situation here, something he believes nobody has ever done before.

◆ 'New technologies' definitely has no written plan. In fact getting to work on new technologies is generally regarded as the plum assignment in Acme (techies get to work on cool stuff and there are no deadlines). The only problem tends to be that people are continuously pulled off working on new technologies to fill gaps on other projects.

◆ The quality system has a plan that the very meticulous HR Manager (who is a former techie and double-jobbing running the quality system) put together.

◆ Training – yes, there is a training plan courtesy of the selfsame, previously mentioned HR Manager.

◆ There is no contingency (as in spare capacity) currently – at least not so far as the CEO is aware – and he would be surprised if project management has been factored into any plan. He therefore declares both of these to be Red (Out of Control).

(4) Calculate the Organizational Performance Indicator (OPI)

Acme's OPI is 2.9 – partway between -1 (the worst) and 5 (the best). At least eight projects are at risk. It's food for thought for the CEO as he turns the page and discovers what he must do next.

SCALING UP/SCALING DOWN

I think it's pretty clear that scaling down this example to a smaller organization simply means that you would end up with a smaller list. As for scaling up for a larger organization, the best way to do this would be to sub-divide it by, say, department or group and then let each one of those do as described above.

AT-A-GLANCE SUMMARY

1. Decide what period of time you want to look at.

2. Make a list of all the projects you are doing or plan to do over that period.

3. Figure out the status of each project.

4. Calculate the Organizational Performance Indicator (OPI).

11

Step 2 – Estimate The Demand

It should really come as no surprise to you that the next couple of steps involve looking at supply and demand. Let's start with the demand.

Now that you've got your list of projects, you must figure out the demand of these projects, i.e. how much work is required to complete each one. Really, there is only one way to do this accurately. That is to estimate each of the projects, as described in Chapter 4 (page 25). But that could take a lot of time and my sense is that, if that was what I now asked you to do, it would be the end of this journey. You'd say, 'Thanks, but no thanks', close the book and that'd be it.

Happily, there are three other ways you could go about estimating the projects. While none of these are as accurate as shown in Chapter 4 and while all projects will eventually have to be estimated properly, the three alternative ways described here have the advantage that they are quick to do. So here they are – your four possibilities for estimating the demand of each of these projects:

1. Estimate the projects as described in Chapter 4 (see page 25).

2. Estimate the projects based on their life cycle.

3. Use the how many people?/how long?/full-time or not? method.

4. Estimate the projects using Small/Medium/Large.

Each method is described in turn.

(1) ESTIMATE THE PROJECTS AS DESCRIBED IN CHAPTER 4

To do this, estimate each of the projects using the estimating method described in Chapter 4 (page 25).

(2) ESTIMATE THE PROJECTS BASED ON THEIR LIFE CYCLE

Sometimes projects consist of a standard set of phases that they go through. Many product development projects, for example, go through phases such as this:

1. Figure out the requirements that the product must satisfy

2. Design it

3. Build it

4. Test it.

Furthermore, the ratio of these phases to each other (i.e. the amount of work involved in each phase compared to the others) tends to be (or should be, if the project is run properly) pretty much the same. So, for example, for the phases above the ratio might be something like this:

Phase	Ratio of work
1. Figure out the requirements that the product must satisfy	1
2. Design it	3
3. Build it	8
4. Test it	4

So if your projects are like this, then this method will work for you provided you know the ratios. How can you know or find out the ratios? Well, just look at a previous project that was completed successfully (assuming there is such a thing!) and get the ratios from that. If you're lucky you'll have records (timesheets, for example) of how much work went into each phase. But if you're not so lucky, you'll just have to work it out as follows.

Get together with some people who worked on or who know about this project. Try to get them to recall how much work went into each phase. They can do this quite simply by trying to remember:

◆ How many people worked in each phase;
◆ For how long; and
◆ Whether or not these people were full-time.

So the conversation might go something like this: 'In the requirements phase, Charlie, Bert and Pete worked on it. Charlie was full-time, the other two probably two days a week. It lasted a month'. So, the total work in this phase then was:

◆ Charlie – 1 person for 1 month full-time=1 man-month;

◆ Bert and Pete – 2 people for 1 month, 4 days a week between them=2 man-months×4/5=8/5=1.6 man-months

So, the total here would be 2.6 man-months.

You would do this for the remaining phases and then extract the ratio. Having done so, you then estimate the first phase of each project (using the how many people?/how long?/full-time or not? method) and apply the ratio to get the other phases.

(3) USE THE HOW MANY PEOPLE?/HOW LONG?/ FULL-TIME OR NOT? METHOD

When there is no common life cycle amongst the projects – or for projects that don't fit into the life cycle, you can use the same method to do the estimation. It'll just take you a bit longer.

◆ How many people worked in each phase?;
◆ For how long?; and
◆ Full-time or not?

(4) ESTIMATE THE PROJECTS USING SMALL/ MEDIUM/LARGE

One final way to come at this problem – it has the advantage of being the quickest, the disadvantage of being the least accurate – is to classify the projects into Small/Medium/Large. People often think in these terms – you often hear them say things like, 'Oh that's a small project' or 'That's going to be a huge project'.

Okay, so if you think one of the projects is 'Small,' try to quantify it using the method.

◆ How many people are working on it?;
◆ For how long?; and
◆ Full-time or not?

This will give you a number of man-months. You can now look at the rest of your list of projects and see if any of the others are roughly of the same size. These are the 'Small' projects.

Now, look at the remaining list. Are all these projects the same size? If yes, try and quantify one of them using the how many people?/ how long?/full-time or not? method. Then all these remaining projects are your 'Mediums'.

If the remaining projects are *not* all the same, try to classify them into 'Medium' and 'Large' – you can have an 'Extra-large' category if you need it. Then quantify each one using the how many people?/how long?/full-time or not? method. You can then estimate the remaining projects by fitting them into one or other of these categories.

However you end up doing it, you will now have estimated all of your projects. Just add all these up to give the overall total. This is the 'demand' (work to be done) for your organization.

EXAMPLE – STEP 2: MEASURE THE DEMAND

The CEO gets some people together to work out the demand – the Head of Product Development and the three Team/Section Leaders. They agree pretty quickly that all of their development projects follow a standard life cycle consisting of four phases. These are:

1. Specification

2. Engineering Development

3. Field Trial

4. Production

This will take care of the bulk of the projects. (We'll see how they deal with the other ones below). They analyse a successful project using the how many people?/how long?/full-time or not? method and establish that their ratio is:

Phase	Ratio of work
Specification	1
Engineering Development	8
Field Trial	1
Production	1

They use this as a guideline but as they go through the projects, they are prepared to modify it for specific circumstances on specific projects.

Since Product Support doesn't follow the standard life cycle, the way they estimate this is as follows: they simply ask how many people they will need over the period they're looking at – remember, it's 18 months – to support existing and new products. The answer they come up with is two people for existing products and three people for new products. This then converts into an estimate of 78 weeks (one and a half years at 52 weeks per year)×the number of people.

New technologies are estimated in exactly the same way. They assume an average of two people in new technologies for the duration. For the quality system they do it like this. There are currently 26 people working on the projects spread between product development (23) and Product Support (3). They plan to hire an additional six people, starting 1 January of the following year.

This will be a total of 32 people. They assume that each of the 32 people involved in the projects will have to spend four days over the 18 months working on the quality system. This gives a figure of 128 person-days and they round this up to 26 person-weeks. For training, they do something similar: they assume 32 people×two weeks training per person, giving 64 person-weeks.

Contingency is calculated at 15 per cent of the total work in the projects and project management at 10 per cent of the total work in the projects. The results of their work are shown below. The total demand is 5,550 man-weeks (Figure 11.1).

SCALING UP/SCALING DOWN
Your list will just be longer or shorter, depending on how many projects you have.

AT-A-GLANCE SUMMARY

1. Estimate each of your projects using any of the four methods:

   ◆ Estimate the projects as described in Chapter 4 (page 25)

   ◆ Estimate the projects based on their life cycle

   ◆ Use the how many people?/how long?/full-time or not? method

   ◆ Estimate the projects using Small/Medium/Large.

   Add up the individual estimates to give the demand.

	THE ACME COMPANY – PROJECT LIST				Work (in MW)
1	**3041**	To finish it			8
	3041				
2		For Sweden			305
3		For France			172
4		For Spain			64
5	**USB Widget**				48
	3141 New architecture				
6		Sweden			312
7		France			64
8		Spain			64
	Stand-alone gizmo				
9		Sweden			232
10		France			68
11		Spain			68
	System-wide device				
12		Sweden			95
13		France			20
14		Spain			20
	NPK 1622				
15		France			720
16		Sweden			128
17		Spain			128
18	**Divergent NPK**				1,032
	CEF				
19		Variant 1			128
20		Variant 2			128
21	**Othert variants**				0
	Product Support				
22		Existing products			156
23		New products			234
24	**New technologies**				156
25	**Quality system**				26
26	**Training**				64
27	**Contingency @**			15%	666
28	**Project management**			10%	444
					5,550
Note:					
'MW' = man-weeks					

Figure 11.1: Acme – Demand

12

Step 3 – Measure The Supply

Now that you've measured the demand, you've got to measure the supply. Here's how to do that:

1. Figure out how many people you have available for projects.

2. For each person, work out how much time they can make available. Get people to do a Dance Card, as described in Chapter 5 (page 41), if you (or they) are in any doubt as to their availability.

3. If you plan to hire any people in the period that you're looking at, repeat (1) and (2) for them. Unsure how many people you're planning to hire? Make some assumption.

4. Add all of these numbers up to give the total.

5. Calculate the Supply-Demand Ratio (SDR).

CALCULATING THE SUPPLY-DEMAND RATIO (SDR)

The OPI was a snapshot of your organization – an assessment at a point in time. There is something else you will need as well:

you must get a sense of how things might evolve in the future. If your snapshot looks good now, will it continue to do so? And if it looks bad, but you feel you can make it better, how likely is that? To answer these and similar questions, you need to look at your organization's Supply-Demand Ratio (SDR).

The SDR of an organization compares the number of people available to work on projects (supply) with the amount of work to be done on those projects (demand). Obviously, given what we said earlier, the supply-demand ration should always be 1. In other words, there should be enough people to do all the work or else the work won't get done. (In my experience, it is rarely if ever 1 – but let's leave that for now.)

The SDR is simply demand divided by supply. I hope you can see the significance of the SDR. If the SDR is less than 1, it means there are more than enough people to do all the work. And if the SDR is equal to 1 there are just enough people to do all the work. But if the SDR is greater than 1 then you're in trouble. It means that even if the OPI showed that all of the projects were Green/on target, the fact that the SDR is greater than 1 means that these projects will *inevitably* start to drift off-target. Let me be clear absolutely clear what I mean by this: it is not that this drifting-off target *might* happen or *sometimes* happens, it is *guaranteed to happen* because of the discrepancy between the supply and the demand.

EXAMPLE – STEP 3: MEASURE THE SUPPLY

The CEO meets with the HR person, the Head of Product Development and the three Team/Section Leaders. They are able to work out the following pretty quickly.

Currently there are 26 people available full-time to work on projects. If we take out four weeks holiday, two weeks public holidays and assume no sickness, then each of these 26 people can contribute 46 weeks' work in a year. So over one and half years, these people will contribute $26 \times 46 \times 1.5 = 1,794$ person-weeks. The six new hires are due to start on 1 January so they will contribute $6 \times 46 = 276$ person-weeks. This gives a total of 2,070 person-weeks.

The SDR = Demand/Supply = 5,550/2,070 = 2.7.

Bad news! In this organization there is 2.7 times more work to be done than there is time and people available to do it.

SCALING UP/SCALING DOWN

For a larger number of people in your organization it will just take you a little bit longer to do the calculations.

AT-A-GLANCE SUMMARY

1. Figure out how many people you have available for projects.

2. For each person, work out how much time they can make available. Get people to do a Dance Card, as described in Chapter 5 (page 41), if you (or they) are in any doubt as to their availability.

3. If you plan to hire any people in the period that you're looking at, repeat (1) and (2) for them.

4. Add all of these numbers up to give the total.

5. Calculate the Supply-Demand Ratio (SDR).

13

Step 4 – Prioritize The Projects

First, an important point – it's another one of those pay-attention-closely moments. I fully accept that there are issues other than having the right amount of people involved in getting projects done. One of key issues is the whole question of skills/knowledge/experience. People are not interchangeable. Different people have different skills/knowledge/experience and the set of skills/knowledge/experience required to do one project is not, in general, the same as that required to do another.

But any talk of skills/knowledge/experience becomes irrelevant if supply and demand are not the same. Only when that problem has been resolved can you start to consider the question of skills/knowledge/experience.

If your supply (from Chapter 12) turns to be greater than or equal to your demand (from Chapter 11), then you're okay – for now! But what if new projects come along to change all that? And if your supply is less than your demand then you've got a real problem. This means that all of the projects are not going to get done. I'll say that again but louder so that you hear it, don't forget it and understand the full significance of it: THIS MEANS THAT ALL OF THE PROJECTS ARE NOT GOING TO GET DONE! And no amount of wishing it were otherwise, pretending that's not what's going to happen, 'JFDI' [a popular management philosophy, (if you can call it that) – stands for 'Just ******* Do It], sweating your resources or anything else is going to make it otherwise.

So now you have a choice. You can decide straight up, right now, which projects are going to get done. Or you can just ignore this uncomfortable fact, go into some kind of denial and let it all roll anyway. Wagons ho! Start projects, make commitments to stakeholders, assign people, start burning budgets – and see what happens. You're not going to decide which projects are going to get done, you'll let Fate handle that decision.

Sounds like a good idea? No, I didn't think so. But if you think it is, then once again, close the book and pass it on to somebody whom you think needs it.

If you think having Fate/luck/chance run your business is *not* a good idea, then it means you're going to decide which projects are not going to be done. In order to do this, you will have to prioritize your projects in some way. Here's how to do that. There are basically two ways:

1. If I could only do one thing, what would it be?

2. Identify the factors making up the prioritization decision.

(1) IF I COULD ONLY DO ONE THING, WHAT WOULD IT BE?

This is as simple as it sounds: you take your list of projects and ask the question, 'If I could only do one project, which one would it be?'

This becomes your number 1 priority. You then take the remaining list and ask the question again. If I could only do one project, which one would it be? This is your number 2 priority. Keep on doing this until the list is prioritized. You can't have a joint priority – a sort of 7(a) and 7(b) – each item is either more important or less important than the other.

(2) IDENTIFY THE FACTORS WHICH MAKE UP THE PRIORITIZATION DECISION

So, what might these factors be? Well, they can be almost anything. Examples would be things like:

◆ Gross profit or savings the project is going to generate.

◆ Who the customer is.

◆ The project produces something that is necessary for longer-term growth/survival.

◆ And so on.

If you're going to use this method, then the best way to do it is like this:

1. Identify the factors that you think are relevant.

2. Decide which is the most important, then the next most important, then the next most important and so on. So, just to take a simple example, you might decide that the identity of the customer is the most important parameter. In other words, you're saying projects for certain customers will always take priority over those of others. Then within that you might decide that gross profit is the most important parameter so you would prioritize your projects thus then:

1. Customer A: Project 1 (Profit=€100,000)

2. Customer A: Project 2 (Profit=€60,000)

3. Customer A: Project 3 (Profit=€50,000)

4. Customer B: Project 1 (Profit=€75,000)

5. Customer B: Project 2 (Profit=€60,000)

6. Customer C: Project 1 (Profit=€70,000)

7. And so on.

It may take you a few reiterations before you get this right. You may do it the first time, look at the result and decide you're really not happy. But that's okay. Put in some additional factor(s) that make(s) it more like the way you think it should be. Eventually, after a handful of reiterations, your prioritization algorithm should settle down.

EXAMPLE – STEP 4: PRIORITIZE THE PROJECTS

The CEO meets with the Head of Product Development and the Head of Sales & Marketing. They eventually prioritize the projects, as shown below. These are some of the issues they run into and this is how they choose to solve them:

◆ They are surprised when 'Product Support – Existing products' comes in at number 1. However, how could it be otherwise? They have to support what is already out in the field – and they get a slice of revenue from this anyway.

◆ There is a lot of argument before 'Quality System' and 'Project Management' get numbers 2 and 3 respectively. The CEO eventually swings it by saying that if 'we're not doing what we're doing right, then there's no point in being in business'. Surely this applies to 'Training' too, the Head of Product Development counters. But the CEO rejects this. There's a lot of stuff they can do with their current staff and current level of training.

PRIORITY	THE ACME COMPANY – PROJECT LIST			Work (in MW)
1	**Product Support – Existing products**			156
2	**Quality system**			26
3	**Project management**		10%	444
4	**Divergent NPK**			1,302
5	**3141**	For Sweden		305
6	**3141 New architecture**	Sweden		312
7	**Stand-alone gizmo**	Sweden		232
8	**3141**	For France		172
9	**NPK 1622**	Sweden		128
10	**NPK 1622**	Spain		128
11	**CEF**	Variant 1		128
12	**CEF**	Variant 2		128
13	**3041**	To finish it		8
14	**3141**	For Spain		64
15	**USB Widget**			48
16	**NPK 1622**	France		720
17	**System-wide device**	Spain		20
18	**3141 New architecture**	France		64
19	**3141 New architecture**	Spain		64
20	**System-wide device**	France		20
21	**System-wide device**	Sweden		95
22	**Stand-alone gizmo**	France		68
23	**Stand-alone gizmo**	Spain		68
24	**Product Support – New products**			234
25	**New technologies**			156
26	**Training**			64
27	**Contingency @**		15%	666
28	**Other variants**			0
				5,550
Note:				
'MW' = man-weeks				

Figure 13.1: Acme's prioritized project list

SCALING UP/SCALING DOWN

Your list will just be longer or shorter, depending on how many projects you have.

AT-A-GLANCE SUMMARY

Prioritize your projects using:

1. If I could only do one thing what would it be?; or

2. Identify the factors that make up the prioritization decision.

14

Step 5 – Make The Cut

If your supply is less than or equal to your demand, then you can probably skip this chapter. But if your demand is greater than your supply, you're probably thinking you can simply increase the supply by adopting the time-honoured technique of getting people to work longer hours. Most bosses and managers seem to think this is a good idea. If you're one of them, think again, comrade!

WHY SUSTAINED OVERTIME IS BAD FOR PRODUCTIVITY

Let's be clear. This is not about a short 'push' to hit a deadline or make a milestone or solve a customer problem, it's about overtime (ten- to sixteen-hour days) over long, sustained periods of time.

Burnout hours are bad because people quickly become less efficient than if they had just worked a normal forty-hour week. While this may sound counter-intuitive, if you think about it then you can see why this would be the case.

Imagine, first of all, that you were going to have the hottest date of your life at 8 p.m. this evening. How would you organize your day? Well, to begin with, you'd probably plan to leave at, say, 5 p.m. For you this would be a hard deadline every bit as vital as having to catch a plane, a train or pick up kids from the crèche. Just to be on the safe side, you might actually plan to have all your work done by 4 p.m. Then, if some genius did come into you late in the day looking for something urgent, you would have an hour's contingency to deal with it.

You would plan your day carefully, figuring out exactly what had to get done so that you could leave by 4 p.m. And you would be brisk with time-wasters, not allowing them to take up much of your time and in the process jeopardize your date. The result would be that the important things would get done and you would be ready by 4 p.m. to go home, scrub up and put your glad rags on to get to your rendezvous.

Now contrast this with if you're coming in to face a day that will last from, say, 8 a.m. to 8 p.m. (or later). And this is not an isolated day. You have been doing this for a long time and, as far as you can tell, will continue to do so for the foreseeable future. Not only that, but you haven't been having weekends or evenings to recover from these days. And maybe you haven't been eating or sleeping very well, or getting much (or any) exercise. And you haven't been seeing too much of your loved ones either. In short, your life has narrowed to being at work, thinking about work, bringing work home with you, or cancelling other things so you can work.

Now, how will you spend your day? Well, you will be lazy with your time. Somebody wants to stop for a chat, you'll be happy to chat with them for ages. You may take long breaks or spend time messing around with your inbox or doing any number of other time-wasting things. This is because you know you have a vast amount of hours to spend each day and if something doesn't get done today then there's always an equally vast number of hours tomorrow. In short, productivity goes out the window.

So, working burnout hours is bad in that it's just not productive. There is lots of attendance but not much achievement – at least not as much as there would be if you were just going home on time. If you want a supporting opinion on this, read *The Deadline*[4], especially Chapter 15.

HOW TO MAKE THE CUT

So now you have to decide what's going to get done and what's not going to get done. Essentially, you have four choices – What, When, Work, Quality. Here they are in turn:

What. Don't do some things at all. The prioritization you did in Chapter 13 (page 118) will enable you to determine which things.

When. Don't do some things in the period of time that you're looking at, i.e. move them off into the future.

Work. Get more people. There are two things you could do here:

1. You could add more people. (But don't forget what we've said previously about adding people to projects.)

2. You might be able to outsource or subcontract some projects. This will obviously add costs because you will have to pay for the subcontracting. Remember too that it won't reduce the work involved in the projects to zero because you will still have to manage the subcontracts.

Quality. There are two aspects to this:

1. Tinker with the quality of what you're doing. The most obvious approach is to cut out or shorten testing or other quality assurance type activities. Not a good idea, I think you'll agree.

2. Find better ways to do things – better tools, methods, procedures.

You are going to find this step to be the most difficult thing you have done so far. Indeed, as the head of an organization that has to deliver to its customers, it's going to be one of the hardest things you will ever do.

But from your point of view, it means you take back the running of your organization from Fate/luck. From your customers' point of view there's a benefit too: they know where they stand. Customers aren't entitled to expect miracles. If they do, it's only because you've given them miracles in the past. But if you continue to deliver miracles, then sooner or later, it will all come horribly unstuck as you run into the unforgiving nature of supply and demand.

So give up miracles and let your customer know how s(he) stands. It's the recipe for a long and happy future for all concerned.

EXAMPLE – STEP 4: PRIORITIZE THE PROJECTS

The CEO meets with the Head of Product Development and the Head of Sales & Marketing. They look at their choices from the list above and come to the conclusion that, in reality, they have the following choices:

◆ They decide that, for them, not doing things at all and not doing things in the next eighteen months amounts to the same thing.

With such a huge gap between supply and demand, not doing certain things will definitely have to be part of their approach.

◆ They can't hire any more full-time people – the budget won't allow it.

◆ They can subcontract certain small projects.

◆ They are not (any longer) going to sweat their resources. The whole idea of this effort has been to find a better way. If this really is a better way, then, by definition, they're going to have to resist the temptation to do this.

◆ They won't tinker with quality.

◆ If they can find better ways to do things, they will.

Having made these decisions, they now look at their prioritized list again (Figure 14.1):

1. They decide that they can subcontract the small project called 'System-wide device' – all three variants, France, Sweden and Spain. Together these projects come to 135 person-weeks. They replace this by a (guessed) figure of four person-weeks to organize and manage the subcontract.

2. It is now clear that some projects are going to have to be dropped. This will reduce the amount of work that goes into 'Product Support – new products'. They decide they will have only two people here – the same as 'Product Support – Existing products' – rather then the three originally planned.

	THE ACME COMPANY – PROJECT LIST			Work (in MW)	Cumulative
PRIORITY					Work (in MW)
1	**Product Support – Existing products**			156	156
2	**Quality system**			26	182
3	**Project management**		10%	444	626
4	**Divergent NPK**			1,302	1,658
5	**3141**	For Sweden		305	1,963
6	**3141 New architecture**	Sweden		312	2,275
7	**Stand-alone gizmo**	Sweden		232	2,507
8	**3141**	For France		172	2,679
9	**NPK 1622**	Sweden		128	2,807
10	**NPK 1622**	Spain		128	2,935
11	**CEF**	Variant 1		128	3,063
12	**CEF**	Variant 2		128	3,191
13	**3041**	To finish it		8	3,199
14	**3141**	For Spain		64	3,263
15	**USB Widget**			48	3,311
16	**NPK 1622**	France		720	4,031
17	**System-wide device**	Spain		20	4,051
18	**3141 New architecture**	France		64	4,115
19	**3141 New architecture**	Spain		64	4,179
20	**System-wide device**	France		20	4,199
21	**System-wide device**	Sweden		95	4,294
22	**Stand-alone gizmo**	France		68	4,362
23	**Stand-alone gizmo**	Spain		68	4,430
24	**Product Support – New products**			234	4,664
25	**New technologies**			156	4,820
26	**Training**			64	4,884
27	**Contingency @**		15%	666	5,550
28	**Other variants**			0	
Note:			Demand =	5,550	
'MW' = man-weeks			Supply =	2,070	

Figure 14.1: Acme – Prioritized list of projects showing cumulative work

3. They realize – and this is a thing that often happens – it's not just a convenience for the author! – that the projects '3141' and '3141 new architecture' (both for Sweden) are essentially the same project. In other words, they have inadvertently double-counted the work here. They replace

it with one project with a slightly higher number of man-weeks. In terms of its status though, they note that they will have to write a new plan for this composite project. This gets them to this (Figure 14.2).

It's still not enough so they have to keep going.

1. Training gets cut completely. The CEO explains the rationale for this. He says that it appears now that for the next eighteen months, Acme is going to have to focus on just delivering its current commitments. There will be little or no work on 'New technologies'. As he says these words he realizes the full implications of this statement. Realistically, there is going to be *no* work on the job 'New technologies' and there will be even less on 'Product Support – New products' so that the figure which they revised only a few minutes ago gets cut further. (They cut it to one person.)

2. They are unable to resist the urge to cut contingency to ten per cent. Their argument is that if this approach is worth its salt, they should need less contingency for unexpected events and firefights.

3. With pain in their hearts, they cut the bottom four (in terms of priority) projects. They are not going to do them. The Head of Sales & Marketing is going to have to square this with any customers. Ooh – that's gonna hurt! They're now at this (Figure 14.3).

But it still isn't enough. They need a big hit to make the numbers work.

PRIORITY	THE ACME COMPANY – PROJECT LIST			Work (in MW)	Cumulative Work (in MW)	STATUS	Red/Amber/ Green/Blue
1	Product Support – Existing products			156	156	Some problems	3
2	Quality system			26	182	On target	5
3	Divergent NPK			1,032	1,214	On target	5
4	3141 New architecture	For Sweden		330	1,544	No written plan	0
5	Stand-alone gizmo	Sweden		232	1,776	On target	5
6	3141	For France		172	1,948	Some problems	3
7	NPK 1622	Sweden		128	2,076	On target	5
8	NPK 1622	Spain		128	2,204	Some problems	3
9	CEF	Variant 1		128	2,332	Out of control	-1
10	CEF	Variant 2		128	2,460	On target	5
11	3041	To finish it		8	2,468	On target	5
12	3141	For Spain		64	2,532	On target	5
13	USB Widget			48	2,580	On target	5
14	NPK 1622	France		720	3,300	Out of control	-1
15	System-wide devices (3)	Spain		4	3,304	Some problems	3
16	3141 New architecture	France		64	3,368	On target	5
17	3141 New architecture	Spain		64	3,432	On target	5
18	Stand-alone gizmo	France		68	3,500	On target	5
19	Stand-alone gizmo	Spain		68	3,568	On target	5
20	Product Support – New products			156	3,724	Some problems	3
21	New technologies			156	3,880	No written plan	0
22	Training			64	3,944	On target	5
			SUBTOTAL	3,944			
27	Contingency @		15%	592		Out of control	-1
3	Project management		10%	394		Out of control	-1
Note:			Demand =	4,930			
'MW' = man-weeks			Supply =	2,070			

Figure 14.2: Acme – First attempt to match supply to demand

4. With even greater pain in their hearts, they pull the plug on 'NPK 1622'. That's really going to hurt them with those customers.

And they're still not there. Finally, the Head of Sales & Marketing's nerve breaks. He freaks out about how difficult it was to land these customers in the first place and now look at what he's going to have to do – go back and tell them that their projects aren't going to happen. These are only estimates – and maybe not very accurate estimates at that. What if the numbers are wrong?

PRIORITY	THE ACME COMPANY – PROJECT LIST			Work (in MW)	Cumulative Work (in MW)	STATUS
1	Product Support – Existing products			156	156	Some problems
2	Quality system			26	182	On target
3	Divergent NPK			1,032	1,214	On target
4	3141 New architecture	For Sweden		330	1,544	No written plan
5	Stand-alone gizmo	Sweden		232	1,776	On target
6	3141	For France		172	1,948	Some problems
7	NPK 1622	Sweden		128	2,076	On target
8	NPK 1622	Spain		128	2,204	Some problems
9	CEF	Variant 1		128	2,332	Out of control
10	CEF	Variant 2		128	2,460	On target
11	3041	To finish it		8	2,468	On target
12	3141	For Spain		64	2,532	On target
13	USB Widget			48	2,580	On target
14	NPK 1622	France		720	3,300	Out of control
15	System-wide devices (3)	Spain		4	3,304	Some problems
16	3141 New architecture	France		0	3,304	On target
17	3141 New architecture	Spain		0	3,304	On target
18	Stand-alone gizmo	France		0	3,304	On target
19	Stand-alone gizmo	Spain		0	3,304	On target
20	Product Support – New products			78	3,382	Some problems
21	New technologies			0	3,382	No written plan
22	Training			0	3,382	On target
			SUBTOTAL	3,382		
	Contingency @		10%	338		Out of control
	Project management		10%	338		Out of control
Note:			Demand =	4,058		
'MW' = man-weeks			Supply =	2,070		

Figure 14.3: Acme – Second pass to match supply to demand

The CEO has some sympathy for his position and this issue of the accuracy of the estimates is worrying him too. What if they *are* wrong? He realizes that they won't have better estimates until they have done proper plans for all of the projects and estimated them, as described in Chapter 4 (page 25). So maybe, he tells the Head of Sales & Marketing, they can put off doing anything with customers until that's been done.

This slightly calms the Head of Sales & Marketing, who had visions of having to be on planes and having very difficult conversations with customers in the next few days. 'So let's estimate and plan these projects properly as a matter of urgency,' says the CEO. 'And also,' he continues, 'let's make a working assumption for the moment that they are correct. Given that it doesn't look like we can cut any more projects,' – the Head of Sales & Marketing emits a loud sigh of relief – 'let's plan to hire three contract people to try and make up the gap. If we can get them in straight away, we'll get three times seventy-eight weeks from them – that's 234 man-weeks.'

Finally, the CEO has one more bright idea. If they're going to be running these projects properly, and if the new quality system is in place, then maybe the incremental increase in product support will be small because the new products will be developed to such a high level of quality. The temptation is too much and they cut 'Product Support – new products' completely.

They call it a day here (Figure 14.4).

The CEO summarizes what this final picture says. They are definitely going to do projects 1–8. The workload here is 2,204 man-weeks. Adding 10 per cent contingency and 10 per cent for project management gives 2,644 man-weeks, but the CEO declares this 'close enough for government work'. They will revisit this when the projects have been estimated accurately.

Projects 9–13 will have to wait pending the estimation of projects 1–8. Then they will see what they will see, the CEO says. At the moment it looks like everything else isn't going to happen, but he's going to wait until projects 1–8 have been estimated to get a sense of the overall accuracy of this exercise.

PRIORITY	THE ACME COMPANY – PROJECT LIST			Work (in MW)	Cumulative Work (in MW)	STATUS
1	Product Support – Existing products			156	156	Some problems
2	Quality system			26	182	On target
3	Divergent NPK			1,032	1,214	On target
4	3141 New architecture	For Sweden		330	1,544	No written plan
5	Stand-alone gizmo	Sweden		232	1,776	On target
6	3141	For France		172	1,948	Some problems
7	NPK 1622	Sweden		128	2,076	On target
8	NPK 1622	Spain		128	2,204	Some problems
9	CEF	Variant 1		128	2,332	Out of control
10	CEF	Variant 2		128	2,460	On target
11	3041	To finish it		8	2,468	On target
12	3141	For Spain		64	2,532	On target
13	USB Widget			48	2,580	On target
14	NPK 1622	France		0	2,580	Out of control
15	System-wide devices (3)	Spain		4	2,584	Some problems
16	Product Support – New products			0	2,584	Some problems
			SUBTOTAL	2,584		
	Contingency @		10%	258		Out of control
	Project management		10%	258		Out of control
Note:			Demand =	3,101		
'MW' = man-weeks			Supply =	2,304		

Figure 14.4: Acme – Third and final pass to match supply to demand

It's as much as they can do right now. They agree to reconvene the meeting in two weeks' time. In the intervening period projects 1–8 will have to be estimated accurately.

Footnote

It may have seemed like I engineered the figures at the Acme Company to provide a particularly dramatic case study. In fact, I didn't. These figures are based on, and not a million miles away from, a real-life situation that I encountered. While it was a severe case of supply-demand imbalance, I'd have to say it wasn't uncommon.

SCALING UP/SCALING DOWN

You'll have more or less work to do depending on how long your project list is and how severe your supply-demand imbalance is. What there is no doubt about is that you'll – potentially – have very difficult decisions to make here.

AT-A-GLANCE SUMMARY

Match supply to demand by doing some combination of the following:

1. **What.** Not doing some things at all.

2. **When.** Not doing some things in the period that you're looking at.

3. **Work.** Either actually adding more people or subcontracting things.

4. **Quality.** Finding better ways to do things.

15

Step 6: Keep It Going

Now that you've done all this work, you just need to keep it going.
You may remember, back in Chapter 10 (page 93), that you did a
'soft audit' of the projects, i.e. you asked the project manager what
the status of the project was and, whatever s(he) said, you took as
being true. In general, when you do this you come up with projects
in a variety of states. Some are on target; some have drifted a bit;
some don't have a plan. If the project manager is very honest with
her/himself, s(he)'ll admit when a project has gone out of control.
So even without going any further, after a soft audit you know that
some projects need to have their planning looked at or, indeed, to be
replanned.

But, as already mentioned, the picture the soft audit gives is rarely
the true one: things are generally worse. And now is the time to
look at all of that. You're going to do two things here:

1. For each project, *starting with the highest priority one and
   working your way down*:

   ◆ Make sure that it has a good plan.

   ◆ Staff the project with as little multitasking as possible.

2. Deal with new projects.

MAKE SURE THAT THE PROJECT HAS A GOOD PLAN

Now, depending on the project's status, do the following:

Red project (Out of control) or Blue project (No written plan)

You need to write a plan as described in the first part of this book (page 23), estimating the project properly. This will return the status of the project to Green.

Amber project (Some problems)

Fix whatever is causing the problems in order to return the project status to Green.

Green project (On target)

Just keep 'em that way!

STAFF THE PROJECTS

Remember as you read this that you're starting with the highest priority project and working your way down the list. Now staff the project fully, i.e. match supply to demand; make sure every job has somebody to do it.

But also do this *with the least amount of multitasking*. In other words, try to ensure that, as far as is humanly possible, everybody working on the project is working on it full-time. This will avoid delays caused by people having to go off to work on other things and then return, having to get their head round the particular project again.

Try to do everything you can to avoid having people multitasking. If the same person is required on several different projects, don't split him/her up! Get him/her to finish one project first and then move on to work on the next one (in the priority list). And there may be other, more creative things you can do. If the same person has to work on several different projects, can you bring somebody in with the same skill set so that you don't have to spread that person across projects? Or can you train somebody else to have the same skill set, or maybe outsource the particular thing?

Ultimately projects will get done more quickly by getting one out of the way and then going on to the next one, rather than by trying to complete several at the same time via multitasking.

DEAL WITH NEW PROJECTS

Things change. New projects come along. Projects once massively important become less so or irrelevant because of changes in the business climate. A new or different project suddenly becomes essential because of something one of our competitors has done. The CEO has a great idea, which actually turns out to be a great idea.

In the old way of doing things, when this happened the new project was just started up and people were pinched from other projects to staff it. Or the suddenly less important one was stripped of most (or all) of its people.

That's not how it will work now.

When an idea for a new project is born it goes onto a list. So too do suggestions about de-prioritizing or changing the priority of projects. Periodically then – once a week, initially if you want to, but it will generally increase to once every two weeks or once a month – the people who decide on such things hold a meeting. At the meetings they:

◆ Consider each project on the list in turn.

◆ Prioritize it.

◆ Fit it into the project priority list.

◆ Make the cut based on this revized priority list, i.e. they drop those projects which can no longer be staffed and only include projects which can be.

REPORT ON THE PROJECTS

This is shown below in the Example.

EXAMPLE

When we last left the Acme company, you may remember they had decided, for definite, to do their top priority projects, numbers 1–8. Here is what these might look like on a plan that the CEO was using to track these projects (Figure 15.1). (For clarity, the detailed entries for Work and Budget are only partly filled in.)

And here is what it might look like a couple of months later with some of the actuals added (Figure 15.2).

And here is what the weekly status reporting for these projects might look like (Figure 15.3).

This report shows everything that everyone would reasonably want to know:

	THE ACME COMPANY – PROJECT TRACKING			Estimated Work (in MW)	Estimated Budget (in €)
PRIORITY					
1	**Product Support – Existing products**			156	312,000
2	**Quality system**			26	52,000
3	**Divergent NPK**			1,032	2,064,000
	– Specification			69	138,000
	– Engineering Development			619	1,238,000
	– Field Trial			206	412,000
	– Production			138	276,000
4	**3141 New architecture**	For Sweden		330	
	– Specification				
	– Engineering Development				
	– Field Trial				
	– Production				
5	**Stand-alone gizmo**	Sweden		232	
	– Specification				
	– Engineering Development				
	– Field Trial				
	– Production				
6	**3141**	For France		172	
	– Specification				
	– Engineering Development				
	– Field Trial				
	– Production				
7	**NPK 1622**	Sweden		128	
	– Specification				
	– Engineering Development				
	– Field Trial				
	– Production				
8	**NPK 1622**	Spain		128	
	– Specification				
	– Engineering Development				
	– Field Trial				
	– Production				
Note:					
'MW' = man-weeks					

Figure 15.1 Project tracking at the organization level

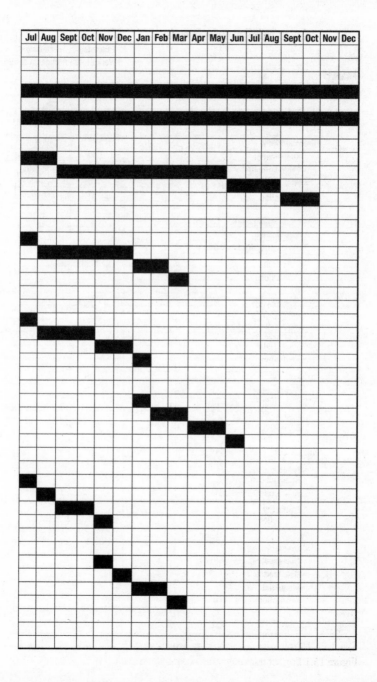

	THE ACME COMPANY – PROJECT TRACKING			Estimated Work (in MW)	Estimated Budget (in €)	Actual Work (in MW)
PRIORITY						
1	Product Support – Existing products			156	312,000	
2	Quality system			26	52,000	
3	Divergent NPK			1,032	2,064,000	127
	– Specification			69	138,000	72
	– Engineering Development			619	1,238,000	55
	– Field Trial			206	412,000	
	– Production			138	276,000	
4	3141 New architecture	For Sweden		330		
	– Specification					
	– Engineering Development					
	– Field Trial					
	– Production					
5	Stand-alone gizmo	Sweden		232		
	– Specification					
	– Engineering Development					
	– Field Trial					
	– Production					
6	3141	For France		172		
	– Specification					
	– Engineering Development					
	– Field Trial					
	– Production					
7	NPK 1622	Sweden		128		
	– Specification					
	– Engineering Development					
	– Field Trial					
	– Production					
8	NPK 1622	Spain		128		
	– Specification					
	– Engineering Development					
	– Field Trial					
	– Production					
Note:						
'MW' = man-weeks						

Figure 15.2 Project tracking showing actuals

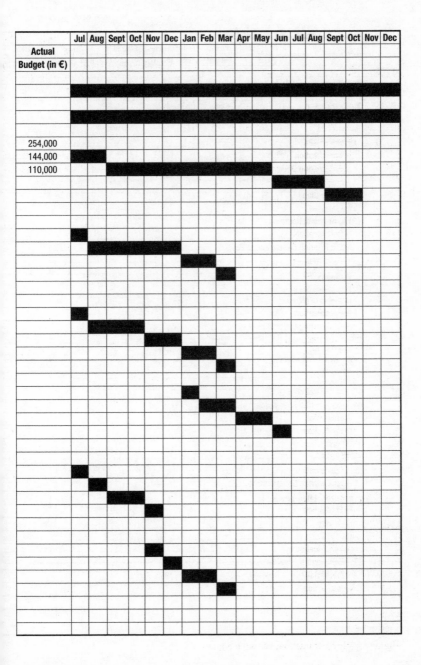

	THE ACME COMPANY – PROJECT TRACKING		Project Manager	Estimated Work (in MW)	Estimated Budget (in €)	Actual Work (in MW)	Actual Budget (in €)
PRIORITY							
1	**Product Support – Existing products**		Charlie	156	312,000		
2	**Quality system**		Fred	26	52,000		
3	**Divergent NPK**			1,032	2,064,000	127	254,000
	– Specification			69	138,000	72	144,000
	– Engineering Development			619	1,238,000	55	110,000
	– Field Trial			206	412,000		
	– Production			138	276,000		
4	**3141 New architecture**	For Sweden	Björn	330			
	– Specification						
	– Engineering Development						
	– Field Trial						
	– Production						
5	**Stand-alone gizmo**	Sweden	Anna	232			
	– Specification						
	– Engineering Development						
	– Field Trial						
	– Production						
6	**3141**	For France	Brigitte	172			
	– Specification						
	– Engineering Development						
	– Field Trial						
	– Production						
7	**NPK 1622**	Sweden	Anna	128			
	– Specification						
	– Engineering Development						
	– Field Trial						
	– Production						
8	**NPK 1622**	Spain	Manuel	128			
	– Specification						
	– Engineering Development						
	– Field Trial						
	– Production						
Note:							
'MW' = man-weeks							

Figure 15.3 Weekly project tracking report

J	A	S	O	N	D	J	F	M	A	M	J	J	A	S	O	N	D	STATUS	STATUS Green/Blue			Change History	Detailed Plan
																			Week 1	Week 2	Week 3	Hyperlink	Hyperlink
																		On target	5	5	5		
																		Some problems	3	3	3		
																		Some problems	3	5	5		
																		On target	5	5	3		
																		On target	5	5	5		
																		No written plan	0	5	5		
																		On target	5	3	5		
																		Some problems	3	3	3		
																			3.6	4.3	4.3		

This week's overall status is there, as well as the historical status, week on week.

All three dimensions are shown – date, work and budget.

Both planned and actual are shown.

If people want to see detailed information, they can follow the hyperlinks to the project's change history or detailed plan.

AT-A-GLANCE SUMMARY

1. For each project, *starting with the highest priority one and working your way down*:

   ◆ Make sure that it has a good plan.

   ◆ Staff the project with as little multitasking as possible.

2. Deal with new projects by revising the priority list and making the cut again.

3. Report on the projects, as described in the previous section (page 137).

Afterword

There, that's all there is to it! As you can see, this is a short book – planning isn't that difficult or that complicated.

But you can also see, I hope, that whether you're just responsible for your own work or you manage a team/group/department/ organization, if you haven't tried proper planning then you really should. It would make a profound difference to not just your working life but to the quality of your life generally.

And wouldn't that be a fine thing indeed?

Good luck with it.

Notes

1. Brooks, Fred, *The Mythical Man-Month*, Addison-Wesley, 1975.

2. Yourdon, Ed, *Death March*, Prentice Hall, 2003.

3. Morrell, Margot and Capparell, Stephanie, *Shackleton's Way: Leadership Lessons from the Great Antarctic Explorer*, Nicholas Brealey Publishing, 2001.

4. DeMarco, Tom, *The Deadline: A Novel About Project Management*, Dorset House, 1997.

Index

ISBN: 978-1-84528-573-9 (paperback)
ISBN: 978-1-84528-574-6 (ebook)
Price: £9.99

'*Top Performance Leadership* is full of good ideas as practiced on
everyone from the Welsh rugby team to the Royal Marines . . . all
are intelligently sketched to form a cohesive and believable model'

People Management

This book examines what is at the core of being a
leader and how to sustain top performance
leadership consistently over time.

ROBINSON

How to Manage
Difficult People

Proven strategies for dealing with
challenging behaviour at work

Alan Fairweather

ISBN: 978-0-71602-398-2 (paperback)
ISBN: 978-1-84803-438-9 (ebook)
Price: £8.99

This book shows you how to identify and understand
awkward and challenging behaviours in others,
and how to manage them.

ROBINSON

ISBN: 978-1-84528-479-4 (paperback)
ISBN: 978-1-84803-699-4 (ebook)
Price: £9.99

What you really need to succeed in business is customers.
Everybody in your business needs to be constantly looking for
them, because you'll always lose some through no fault of your
own. But few people are naturally comfortable with selling –
and not everyone has been trained to do so.

This clear, memorable and easy to understand book
contains practical information on how to do it right –
and how to do it better if you are already doing it.

ROBINSON